About Quantum Books

Quantum, the unit of emitted energy. A Quantum Book is a short study distinctive for the author's ability to offer a richness of detail and insight within about one hundred pages of print. Short enough to be read in an evening and significant enough to be a book.

To Irrigate a Wasteland

JOHN W. MACY, JR.

To Irrigate a Wasteland

The Struggle to Shape a Public Television System in the United States

UNIVERSITY OF CALIFORNIA PRESS
BERKELEY · LOS ANGELES · LONDON

University of California Press
Berkeley and Los Angeles, California
University of California Press, Ltd.
London, England

ISBN: 0-520-02498-2
Library of Congress Catalog Card Number: 73-81200
Printed in the United States of America

*Dedicated to the men and women
who apply their talents to the cause
of public television*

Contents

vii

Contents

Foreword

Edward R. Murrow once said of television: "This instrument can teach, it can illuminate; yes, it can even inspire. But it can do so only to the extent that humans are determined to use it to those ends. Otherwise, it is merely lights and wires in a box."

John W. Macy, Jr. is one of those humans determined to use broadcasting to teach and illuminate and even inspire. His Gaither Lectures cover an exceedingly important chapter in the history of American broadcasting. For many reasons, I find it a special honor to have been asked to write a foreword to their publication. First, John and I are old friends who served together in the Kennedy Administration. Second, we have worked together in public broadcasting in my role as chairman of WTTW, the public television station in Chicago. Finally, while I was not privileged to know Rowan Gaither, I later followed in his path at the Rand Corporation; the lectures bearing his name are of exceptional distinction.

As I write these words, we are engaged in a crisis in public broadcasting. Just a week ago, as a representative of the Public Broadcasting Service, I attended meetings in Washington with John Macy's successor at the Corporation for Public Broadcasting. Our discussions failed to reach an agreement on working relationships between the Corporation and the local stations—and the fundamental issues discussed in these lectures remain unresolved.

It is astonishing and discouraging that our country has not yet found a way to develop a first-class noncommercial broadcasting service. When one travels to Europe or to Japan, it is apparent that other nations are decades ahead of us in harnessing the potential of broadcasting with noncommercial values. We started late in the United States, and we still have a long way to go to match the achievements of other systems.

Yet, in reading the lectures, I have reflected about our steady progress in the last decade. When I went to the FCC in 1961, I was amazed to find that there was no public television station in New York, or Los Angeles, or Philadelphia, or Washington, or Baltimore, or Cleveland, or many other large cities. There was no network connecting the few existing stations, and the audience was painfully small. There was no "Sesame Street," no "Electric Company," no "Book Beat," no "Firing Line." Today, although we have not progressed far enough, or fast enough, we do have millions of viewers who care deeply about public broadcasting. We have more than two hundred stations and we do have a network. Despite present obstacles, public broadcasting is destined to grow and prosper and enrich our lives.

For carrying on the good fight in an effective, straightforward, and highly principled way, John Macy merits the respect and thanks of a generation of Americans who have benefited and will benefit from his work. Under John's leadership, public broadcasting remained nonpolitical and independent. He did irrigate the wasteland, and the seeds left by that irrigation left roots which will grow, flourish, and prevail. It is essential that others now take up John Macy's high standard if we are to fulfill the vision of E. B. White expressed in his wise words about television:

Noncommercial television should address itself to the ideal of excellence, not the idea of acceptability—which is what keeps commercial television from climbing the staircase. I think television should be the visual counterpart of the literary essay, should arouse our dreams, satisfy our hunger for beauty, take us on journeys, enable us to participate in events, present great drama and music, explore the sea and the sky and the woods and the hills. It should be our Lyceum, our Chautauqua, our Minsky's, and our Camelot. It should restate and clarify the social dilemma and the political pickle. Once in a while it does, and you get a quick glimpse of its potential.

Newton N. Minow

I

To Design and Construct a Viable System in the Public Interest

When Newton Minow delivered his first address as chairman of the Federal Communications Commission (FCC) in early 1961, he coined a description of the current television offerings that still aptly applies to the bulk of programming today, a dozen years later. "The vast wasteland" he painted for the National Association of Broadcasters (NAB) that day has continued to attract ever larger American audiences and has gained ever mounting influence in the lives of all its viewers. According to 1971 audience data published by the National Association of Broadcasters, in the average home, television is watched for five hours and fifty minutes a day. To give this massive viewing a slightly different statistical twist, the average family spends the equivalent of twelve full weeks out of the year in front of that one-eyed monster. The only activity, in fact, that occupies more time in the home is sleeping—although some would observe that the two pastimes are synonymous.

These numbers constitute a rising, not a falling, trend. That figure of five hours, fifty minutes represents the seventh consecutive year of increase in average viewing time per day. These habitual viewers are located in more than sixty million homes—homes in Watts and White

Plains, in Kalamazoo and San Francisco, homes in the Kentucky hills and the canyons of Manhattan. If the facts were available to us, I suspect we could prove that Americans in the past year have spent more time watching TV than all Americans since Plymouth Rock have spent reading books.

It is a well-watched wasteland. The audience is there. How much more benefit in enlightenment and pleasure that audience could receive if that wasteland could be irrigated! New vistas with new and different blossoms could offer enrichment of mind and spirit from those hours invested in watching. The landscape could be planted with program substance that would enhance learning in the unique way in which the visual medium can present it. The passivity that can fall upon the viewer from his endurance test with the tube can be overcome by provocative and topical images that raise interest and promote involvement.

To irrigate a wasteland has been an objective of many leaders in the past twelve years, but particularly of those who have struggled in recent times to shape a public television system in the United States. The design and construction of such a system to serve the interests of the American people in this potent and influential area of communications has become a national goal. This endeavor, undertaken at a late stage in the medium's development, has faced critical political and financial, artistic and organizational difficulties in moving toward this goal. The difficulties persist to this day. They will undoubtedly persist into the future as a new institution, without precedent or prototype, emerges from the dynamics of the broadcasting world. No static institution can ever meet the public service interest or potential.

The thrust for this irrigation project was formed by the Public Broadcasting Act of 1967 and the creation of a newly chartered, unique, nonprofit corporation, substantially funded by the federal government but not a federal agency—the Corporation for Public Broadcasting (CPB).

The analysis and observations that follow are drawn from my privileged experience as the first president and chief executive officer of that corporation. Since resigning from that post in September 1972, I have had the opportunity to reflect, in moderately objective contemplation, upon the struggle to create this system. I welcomed this series of four lectures as an opportunity to translate these thoughts into a written record that may serve to more fully inform the American citizen about the system designed to broaden his choice, to illuminate the issues of the times, to reflect the cultural treasures, and to provide improved public service during the hours of viewing.

I realize that my discussion will constitute the 1973 edition of this series honoring Rowan Gaither and devoted to the central theme of system analysis. Although my variation on that theme may be unduly electronic and more political than analytical, I will attempt to follow the worthy tradition established by my predecessors in the series—the distinguished president of the University of California, Charles Hitch, and those champions from the Brookings stable, Charles Schultz and Alice Rivlin.

FROM SYSTEM TO SYSTEM

My qualifications to deal with this theme were pointed up by a public broadcasting associate who, when commenting on my decision to resign from the CPB presidency, described my tenure as "an effort to convert a system (small "s") into a System (large "S")." This comment also reflected the mid-stage in the development of public service television at which CPB entered the scene. This was not, and could not be, a *de novo* undertaking. The basic elements—the local TV stations with licenses from the FCC—were in being and increasing in number. Preliminary moves toward a national service had been initiated. Patterns of collaboration on the basis of region, type of station, and common program interests had been formed. A history of noncommercial, educational, and public television had already run for nearly fifteen years when this lift from lower to upper case in system construction was launched.

At the time he sighted the wasteland in that April 1961 speech to the National Association of Broadcasters, Newton Minow asserted that in today's world, "in a time of peril and opportunity, the old complacent, unbalanced fare of action-adventure and situation comedies is simply not enough." Continuing in a hopeful and constructive vein in the same speech, he challenged TV leadership— "when television is good, nothing—not the theater, not the magazine or newspaper—nothing is better." At that point he turned to educational broadcasters to provide "the better" as well as the program variations. He urged them to seek systematic growth. He promised support by saying, "if there is not an educational television system in this country, it will not be the fault of the FCC." So, the man who identified the wasteland shared the belief that what became known as *public* television represents the chief promise that something can indeed be done to make television blossom.

PUBLIC RADIO

The roots of public broadcasting reach back more than fifty years to the first radio stations that took to the air from university physics or engineering laboratories. The first radio station of any kind to broadcast back in 1919 was educational and was located in the laboratories of the University of Wisconsin at Madison. In the following decade other pioneers at state universities joined that station on the air, and as they multiplied they formed electronic extension services for the scattered audiences with crystal sets.

But the development of radio along commercial lines, after the stampede for frequency allocations, soon submerged most of these audio efforts at public service. Prior to the establishment of the FCC by the Communications Act of 1934, the Federal Radio Commission (FRC) had been created in 1927 to provide governmental regulation in frequency assignment and to apply the standard of "public interest, convenience, and necessity" in licensing stations. Even the 1934 Act gave no recognition to educational, noncommercial radio stations but directed the FCC to study the possibility of allocating fixed percentages of such facilities and to report back to Congress the following year. But the FCC recommended no such special assignments—it presumed that time would be available for such broadcasts on the regular commercial frequencies because those stations were obliged to air public service programs. Only when FM assignments arose in 1945 did the commission alter this position. Twenty FM channels were allocated in a special classification to be used exclusively for noncommercial educational broadcasting.

This allocation was liberalized in 1948 to stimulate greater use of FM frequencies by very low power stations. This action permitted a decided increase in educational stations.

Only about twenty-five educational stations survived through the decades to broadcast on the AM band. Most of these licenses were issued to schools and universities, and these stations had limited power, only ten watts, so their service range tended to be campus-bound. Their close tie-in with educational institutions meant that their hours, days, and weeks of broadcasting were restricted. Thus, the present number of more than five hundred licensees gives a misleading impression of the scope and impact of public service radio—at least until the advent of CPB.

But the recent moves toward system development in public radio call for separate analysis in a separate volume. This turn-away from radio is not intended as a put-down of the public service potential of the older medium. Radio was properly included under the terms of the Public Broadcasting Act of 1967 and the developmental aegis of CPB. It has experienced marked growth and has extended its reach and its programming as a consequence. The Corporation for Public Broadcasting set eligibility standards of power, broadcast time, and community service. Under those standards a broader public service has become available to listeners through an increasing number of stations —63 in 1969 and 124 in 1972.

The medium can be much more effective than television for some types of programs. Many a TV talk show or symphony orchestra concert are really radio programs with pictures. Radio production costs are much lower— about 10 percent of television costs per time unit for the same type of programs.

Further, there are three hundred million radio sets—one and one-half per man, woman and child in this country—with a high degree of portability for a mobile population. They can be ubiquitous receivers for the public message, even with the reduced availability from the FM band. I will, however, refrain from making the case for public radio now. Suffice it to say that I recognize its progress and its potential, but its history and current health provide only limited guidance in relation to the development of a public television system.

RESERVATION OF CHANNELS

The loss of frequencies to almost exclusive commercial allocation in radio was not repeated in television but was avoided only after a prolonged campaign fought by the advocates of educational broadcasting. The initial allocation of television channels by the FCC on the VHF (Very High Frequency) band (channels 2 to 13) gave absolutely no consideration to channels for noncommercial educattional purposes. This oversight was identified, however, and an intensive lobbying effort was mounted by educators and public service supporters during an extended but temporary allocation freeze between September 1948 and April 1952. Under the banner of the Joint Council on Educational Television, these forces concentrated their fire on the FCC, where they found a champion in Commissioner Frieda Hennock. Finally, in April 1952, the commission issued the vital reservation authority which designated 242 channels (80 VHF and 162 UHF [Ultra High Frequency]) for the exclusive use of educational stations.

At that time, all available channels in the VHF band were already allotted. This was particularly true in the largest markets and where metropolitan areas were in close proximity to each other. Consequently, most of the noncommercial reservation was placed in the UHF (channel 14 and up) band, in the belief that such channels would provide equal quality reception to those in VHF. This has never been true.

Even after the passage of legislation requiring all sets to be manufactured with UHF capability, the tuning of UHF channels was difficult and unreliable. One exhausted public television devotee claimed he had been required to develop "safecracker's fingers" in order to receive the UHF station. The presence of the commercial channels on VHF further disadvantaged the noncommercial station on UHF. To many casual viewers, the noncommercial station was UHF and hard to get, while the commercial station was VHF and easy to get.

This disadvantage was felt with greatest pain where it existed in the largest markets with the highest potential audience. Noncommercial television stations in cities like Los Angeles, Washington, Detroit, Cleveland, Cincinnati, and Kansas City are handicapped to this day by their presence in UHF, where VHF stations in Boston, New York, Chicago, Philadelphia, and San Francisco are aided by their placement in VHF, within the reach of a much larger audience. Pleadings at the FCC have been unavailing, because its members are unwilling to admit publicly that UHF is not just as good as VHF. The Washington station is presently seeking an experimental license to test a VHF channel, as an alternative to Channel 26, at a dial position between existing adjacent channels in the same market. The approval of this experiment by the FCC could afford the first real test of the long-standing requirements for spacing between stations and could possibly lead to more effective use of the spectrum. However, if the FCC decision-making goes at the traditional speed new technological advances may overtake the research before it is ever conducted.

A different approach has been promoted by public television leaders in Los Angeles. There, funds have been raised on more than one occasion to purchase one of the seven commercial VHF channels. But each time the $15 to $22 million has been raised, the selling price has escalated to a new high, and the public station in the second largest market remains at Channel 28. This purchase method followed the precedent of New York where channel 13 was acquired in 1962 for more than $13 million.

EDUCATIONAL ROLE OF TELEVISION

The potential educational contribution of television was the prime motivation for noncommercial license applications. School systems and universities were attracted to the medium for instructional purposes. They believed that talented instructors could reach larger student populations through television, that the substance of instruction might be enriched, and that possibly the increases in instructional budgets—in the face of rising enrollments—might be restrained. Although some planners foresaw audiences gaining viewing benefits outside the classroom, the principal justification was classroom use. Most licensees originally founded their broadcast schedule on that area of service. Teachers were generally less than enthusiastic about the invasion of the monster; for many years unused sets were discovered in school closets and classrooms. But even today a significant percentage of total broadcast hours (35 percent) is designed and transmitted by local stations for instructional purposes. Many stations cling to the educaional label to preserve that instructional identity in opposition to the broader program range inferred by the term *public*.

This educational objective brought educational institutions, mostly public but some private, into the intricate and complicated management of television licenses. The first station on the air in 1953 was KUHT on Channel 8 in Houston, as a licensee of the University of Houston. The governing board and president of that institution were granted that necessary license and started producing and transmitting school programs to the community. KUHT became a forerunner of one of four types of broadcasting stations in the noncommercial system; the university type. In time, the pioneer radio station at the University of Wisconsin had a television brother with the same call letters. From Orono, Maine and Tampa, Florida to Honolulu, Hawaii, and College, Alaska, more than forty universities entered the television business, each with its own variation in the pattern of governance and with widely varying support and interest on the part of the chief executive. In some instances, the university president was actively involved in securing a strong community position for the station and necessary financial priority in university fund raising. At the other extreme, some stations were buried in the speech or communications departments and were virtually invisible to institutional leadership and in annual budgets until some regent or influential citizen objected to broadcast content.

SCHOOL BOARD STATIONS

A second category of station in the educational field was that governed by the local school board. Although this pattern has not enjoyed much recent expansion, it was a natural consequence of the instructional emphasis and the possession of radio licenses by school boards. Examples among the twenty-three stations in that group are the Charlotte-Mecklenburg County School Board ownership of the station in Charlotte, North Carolina, and the Jefferson County School Board in the Louisville, Kentucky viewing area. In these cases, the board and the superintendent have been obliged to deal with the management and program problems of the station. Serious public policy issues faced these boards and officials in other areas, and so their attention to station development has been peripheral and marginal at best. The ETV station's expensive appetite for plant, equipment, and talent has been viewed as an added burden of serious proportions when school bond issues were being defeated and teachers were striking for increased pay. At the same time, the station's courtship of other community sources of support might be prohibited by statute or viewed as dilutions of responsibility. Like the public university stations, these stations were dependent for the most part on local tax revenues for survival.

STATE SYSTEMS

The pattern of statewide educational television (ETV) systems has spread out of the southeast and across the country as the third type of station organization. The concept of delivering instructional service to all schools within the boundaries of the state from a single production center has become increasingly attractive. Each state has evolved its own unique arrangement. No national uniformity has been applied. In some states, a special agency has been created to govern the system. In others, the existing department or board of education has accepted the task. And in some states, the state educational television system has become an extension of the university system. Perhaps the most complete system operates in the state of South Carolina, where a special board governs it. The South Carolina system completely covers the state with both over-the-air transmitters and closed circuit saturation, and it receives programs beamed for instructional use in elementary and secondary schools, the police precinct stations, hospital training rooms, and citizens' homes.

In other southern states—North Carolina, Georgia, Alabama, Mississippi, and most recently Louisiana—ETV has been nurtured with state revenue to build an electronic supplement to public education. Legislators and educational leaders have joined to support use of this mode of technical development to overcome longtime educational deficiencies. In Kentucky, a system of eleven transmitters is programmed from a modern broadcasting plant on the edge of the state university at Lexington. The system carries educational fare to children in the cities and Appalachian mountain communities. An equally comprehensive system has recently been augmented in Nebraska through higher education curriculum broadcast throughout the state.

Where stations already existed through university, school board, or community initiative, they have been linked for statewide coverage by an independent board (Pennsylvania) or by the state university (New York). For several hours each day, the long distance telephone lines or microwave systems tie these independent stations together for the delivery of school services or—with increasing frequency in recent times—to carry other public services, such as live telecasts of the state legislature or reports from the governor.

The state as a broadcast unit has been efficient and manageable. The employment of statewide television has already strengthened the effectiveness of state services and may well constitute a major influence in developing the modern role of state government. Virtually every state has such systems already operating or at the planning stage. Previously developed plans have aborted in some states, and others have suffered from political crisis or financial anemia, but the trend continues to move in this direction.

THE COMMUNITY STATIONS

The best known design for educational stations, however, has been the so-called community model which has emerged in major metropolitan areas—Boston, Chicago, San Francisco, Los Angeles, Pittsburgh, Cleveland, Washington, Philadelphia, New York, and Dallas. The history of each of the more than forty licensees is different, but the initiative has always come from one or a few civic leaders who were attracted to the medium as a form of public service and as an alternative to commercial programs. In most instances these leaders were able to tap financial resources in the corporate, foundation, or educational worlds to supplement effective drives for contributions from viewers.

In a real sense, these stations have been launched and supported by voluntary giving and have been less dependent on public appropriations from educational or other spigots. Their boards of governance have been dominated, until recently, by those who have the time and interest to guide community enterprise of a not-for-profit nature. Such people are accustomed to making things happen through voluntary citizen action. They have been less committed to programs confined to instructional goals and have ventured into cultural and journalistic offerings from local sources or elsewhere. Although these stations are determined to meet the unique needs of the community to which they are licensed, they have also been in the lead in seeking broadcast material which can only flow from national investment and production. They have been inclined to seek each other's products to extend their reach and enlarge their audience, and they are eager to share their home-produced programs with the rest of the system.

The absence of large and regular transfusions of public funds has provided an uncertain but independent state of health for these stations. The vagaries of voluntary fund raising, combined with the high cost of capital facilities and program production, have created perpetual tensions and economic brinksmanship. But the viewer's dollar has lessened the possibility of political intervention over program selection and has increased the sense of citizen participation and response.

KEY ROLE OF THE STATION MANAGER

The key figures in the guidance of these separate and independent stations were not the board members, as important and supportive as they were, but the station managers who accepted day-to-day responsibility for these public service instruments. Appointed by their boards, they came from teaching, broadcasting, business, and public administration. Some had been engineers, others fund raisers and public relations specialists, and still others had operated in production studios. They assumed managerial assignments of complexity and diversity. They frequently faced infinite expectations with tightly restricted resources. Their knowledge of the product was initially narrow, and those from commercial television frequently were motivated by visions of creative freedom beyond the range of accomplishment. They soon sought the protective fellowship and mutual assistance of association in a variety of organizations.

The National Association of Educational Broadcasters (NAEB) was a natural rallying point for such association at the national level. It became a center for new, collective efforts to share program sources, to lobby for federal assistance, and to discuss the shared agonies of station operation. To focus attention on the ETV managers' needs, a special division of the association, Educational Television Stations (ETS), was formed in the 1960s and became a political force for its members in the evolving formation of the system.

REGIONAL ALLIANCES

The community of interest among station managers was also manifest in the establishment of regional groupings with new alphabetical combinations. The most ambitious endeavor of this nature was the Eastern Educational Network (EEN) which, under the leadership of Hartford Gunn, the manager of the Boston station, constituted an alliance of more than thirty stations in the northeast. Dollar and program contributions to the alliance made possible a bona fide network with dedicated telephone lines throughout the area. The cooperative form of mutual assistance raised the quality and widened the diversity of program choices available to supplement purely local production. The combined funding permitted production of more elaborate and appealing instruction materials for possible use by member stations in meeting local educational needs. No two regional combinations were identical. None were as ambitious or politically potent as EEN.

Operating out of a strong base at Columbia, South Carolina, SECA (Southern Educational Communications Association) brought together stations stretching from Maryland to Texas for a weekly prime time regional program and for managers' meetings to discuss common problems. In the Great Lakes area, CEN (Central Educational Network) was particularly active in promoting self-training sessions on issues of current controversy as well as producing occasional program contributions. In contrast, the regional network called Midwestern Educational Television (MET) was almost a private interconnection controlled by the St. Paul station for other stations in Minnesota and the Dakotas.

The prime objective of the Rocky Mountain Corporation for Public Broadcasting (RMCPB), established following the activation of CPB, was to secure time delay for that time zone in that sparsely served area. Only six stations in the region were on the air in 1969, and Montana and Wyoming remain today the only states with no educational licensees. They attempted to work with the regional confederation of governors to achieve broader mutual assistance in program production and distribution.

To be totally different, the West Coast group of stations sustain two regional entities: the Western Educational Network (WEN) and Western Radio–Television Association (WEST). The former is the western counterpart of the regional impulse for an association of stations without its own interconnection or regional program production. The latter is the evolutionary result of stations' efforts to stage an annual meeting intended for those not rich enough to attend national conventions, which are usually held in the east. Both organizations exist today in a state which one knowledgeable ETV veteran described as "a rather uneasy mutuality."

No organizational portrait of ETV would be complete without a description of the prominent role of the Ford Foundation. From the earliest days, the foundation was a major source of support for the infant stations and their emerging systems. Through its subsidiary, the Fund for Adult Education, matching grants were provided to the first thirty stations to launch their broadcasts. Without these incentives, more time would have been lost in the early development stage, or possibly no development at all would have occurred.

This form of capital assistance was supplemented by the creation of the National Educational Television and Radio Center (NET) as the first national element in the system. Originally NET was intended to offer a library service for all stations, to extend their program inventory beyond local production capability. This initial function was expanded, in response to collective station requests, to encompass station support activities. With augmented funding from the Ford Foundation and occasional underwriting (a nonprofit definition of sponsorship without advertising) from private corporations, NET enlarged its program production role to approximately ten hours of programs each week, roughly divided into equal parts of cultural and public affairs. These programs were distributed by mail—bicycled, in the quaint jargon of the broadcasters—to stations which became affiliates of NET through an agreement not too dissimilar to the network-local station agreements in commercial broadcasting. The NET president, John White, who had been an educational broadcaster in Pittsburgh, became a leading spokesman for all educational stations as well as for NET, and he continued to broaden the services of his organization as needs were identified.

The important contribution by NET to station schedules received mixed reactions from local stations. Some applauded the new and diversified fare offered, and others complained of "New York taste" or "liberal political bias" and demanded more station participation or even control in program selection. The dissent generated yet another organization, the NET Affiliates Council. Meeting several times a year with NET management, this group of elected station managers reflected local views. All station managers gathered annually as affiliates and added yet another meeting to the crowded travel calendar of station managers.

The central arch of the system, such as it was, could only exist through the continuing commitment of the Ford Foundation, which had invested more than $150 million in educational television by the mid-1960s. As is true of a rich and generous uncle, the largesse of the foundation attracted little affection from its beneficiaries. The foundation's motives were suspect. Its objectivity was challenged. There were those critics who believed only the federal government should play such a central role in the development of a national system. It was claimed by some that foundation money was really tax money anyway. Foundation money, exempt from taxation, was money to be invested in causes judged to be appropriate by a board outside of public accountability. Even those appreciative of the foundation's support realized that its wealth would

commission. With active support in the administration from John Gardner (secretary of HEW), Leonard Marks (director of USIA), and Douglass Cater (presidential assistant), the proposal gained the presidential endorsement. But it was decided that private funds rather than federal appropriations would underwrite the work of the commission. The Carnegie Corporation assumed this role, and a commission of outstanding citizens was named, with James Killian, an experienced leader of such public policy study groups, as chairman. From his days as President Eisenhower's science advisor, Killian was familiar with the federal scene. In addition, there was no doubt about the interest of President Johnson, a former teacher and broadcast enthusiast, in the work of the commission, even though private funding placed it outside of government. He was personally involved in the selection of some commission members. Two of his top assistants, Cater and Marks, were always available to the commission in the course of its study. And the previous association of his Secretary of Health, Education, and Welfare with the Carnegie Corporation provided yet another link between the administration and the commission.

CARNEGIE COMMISSION—1966

Much of 1966 was devoted to the Carnegie Commission's exploration and discussion of educational television. The basic policy and structural issues were analyzed at both commission and staff levels. Killian committed time and skill to preparation and leadership of monthly meetings. To assure input from the licensees, ninety-two local ETV stations in thirty-five states were visited. Possible foreign models in Great Britain, Japan, Canada, Italy, Germany,

Russia, and Sweden received firsthand scrutiny. The views of every public and private organization with even indirect involvement were sought and evaluated.

This stage in the legislative process was successfully concluded in a virtually unanimous report entitled: Public Television, a Program for Action. That report represented a blueprint for subsequent legislation and administrative action. In fact, in later years that report gained the sanctity of holy writ and attracted interpreters who selectively cited its concepts and phrases to support widely differing views.

The fundamental conclusion in the final report of the commission was an affirmation of the public service benefits of educational television and of the public policy desirability of federal support. In its opinion: "A well-directed educational television system, substantially larger than the existing system and far more pervasive and effective, must be brought into being if the full needs of the American public were to be served."

To advance this cause the commission report recommended:

1) concerted efforts at all levels to improve facilities, increase the number of stations, and provide adequate support for existing stations;

2) creation by Congress of a *federally chartered, non-profit, nongovernmental* corporation, the Corporation for Public Broadcasting (CPB), empowered to receive and disburse governmental and private funds to extend and improve programming;

3) that CPB support at least two national production centers and contracts with independent producers in program development;

4) that CPB support local programs by local stations for their own and for "more than local use";

5) that CPB provide live interconnection by conventional (Bell system) means, while exploring future use of satellite

technology, and that preferential rates or free service be considered where the law did not prohibit these;

6) that CPB support research and development to improve program production and technical experimentation to improve present television technology;

7) that CPB provide means for recruitment and training of technical, artistic, and specialized personnel;

8) that Congress provide federal funds required by CPB through a manufacturer's excise tax on the sale of television sets and through a separate trust fund; and

9) that HEW support expanded facilities assistance to achieve nationwide coverage.

The central thrust of the commission proposal was the organizational device of the new corporation. In fact, the commission considered this such a fundamental recommendation that other actions were proposed on the condition that the corporation be created.

The commission sidestepped instructional broadcasting and educational technology and concentrated on more general or, as they originated the term, *public* television. That description brought the term into currency not only for the title of the corporation but as the label for the system that it would seek to develop.

The relationship of the program distribution process with the stations was a critical area of advice in light of subsequent controversy as to whether the process was too centralized or had become "a fourth network," imitating the three commercial networks. This issue had already produced tensions between NET, the national program producer and distributor, and the stations. The commission affirmed the view that public television needed both national and local inputs and that adequate safeguards should be constructed to preserve the autonomy of the local producing agencies. In view of the later semantic tussles over the definitions of "interconnection" and "networking," this commission comment in the final report is interesting although not particularly definitive:

The commission consequently proposes that public television look to interconnection primarily as a device for the distribution of programs. Whatever is produced within the system would be transmitted over the interconnection, according to a schedule made known in advance to station managers. There would be no expectation that the programs would be immediately rebroadcast by the local station (although of course there would be nothing to prevent such use). Instead, the local station manager would be expected to record those programs he might later use, ignoring the rest.

If the innovative idea of the corporation was the paramount recommendation, the treatment of the federal financing problem was a close second. Subsequent history has bracketed these two proposals in ever closer relationship. The commission members wrestled with this issue throughout their deliberations. They were concerned over the potential influence of federal money on independent programming, particularly in the sensitive area of video journalism. The political characteristics of the annual budget and appropriations process raised the spector of congressional intervention against the funding of programs without universal appeal. The dependence of the system on the uncertainties inherent in the annual cycle would handicap planning. The importance of massive federal funds in nationwide growth could be eroded by the traditional pattern of annual increments related to past levels of spending or unrelated fiscal trends. The objective was to design a method of funding that would be related to the viewer's stake in the public medium and that could provide regular, long-term revenue with rising amounts and public accountability.

The possible options were discussed but not deeply researched. The recommendation for a dedicated excise tax on the sale of sets was the preferred course, although there remained doubt about its political feasibility. At least it would constitute independent funding, outside of the annual appropriation, on a regular and assured basis.

The public interest vision in the commission's report was summed up in a paragraph by Jack Gould in the *New York Times* of January 27, 1967:

The commission sees television as the electronic age's extension of the library and art center, the platform of opportunity for the politician, writer, analyst, actor, humorist, scientist, choreographer, and teacher. In the cross-fertilization of multiple minds, the group feels, can come a clue to an interrelated society, the acid test of positive citizenship. In short, the limitless riches of the intellectual, artistic, and social substance of a culture are the ingredients awaiting imaginative and professional conveyance to the home screen under circumstances where the event shapes the medium and not vice versa.

PRESIDENTIAL ACTION—1967

The spotlight shifted to the executive for the next stage. Prepublication copies of the commission report gained support from the president and his advisors, as evidenced by the State of the Union commitment in January 1967:

We shall develop educational television into a vital public resource to enrich our homes, educate our families and to provide assistance in our classrooms. We should insist that the public interest be fully served through the public's airwaves.

I will propose these measures to the 90th Congress.

And so he did, in a message on education and health a few weeks later. Calling for the enactment of a Public Television Act of 1967, Johnson requested the Congress to:

increase federal funds for television and radio construction to $10,500,000 for fiscal year 1968, a threefold increase; create a Corporation for Public Broadcasting authorized to provide support to noncommercial television and radio; and provide $9 million in fiscal year 1968 as initial funding.

As though anticipating a question about the missing provision for long-range financing, the message went on to state: "Next year, after careful review, I will make further proposals for the Corporation's long-range financing." President Johnson coupled this commitment with these words of public principle: "Noncommercial television and radio in America, even though supported by federal funds, must be absolutely free from any federal government interference over programming."

The proposed bill was drafted in HEW, with close White House participation. It entered the heavy flow of Great Society proposals moving toward Capitol Hill from the president. Although congressional enthusiasm for social reform had begun to flag with the reduced Democratic margin from the 1966 election and the preoccupation with the Vietnam war, the legislative climate and timing were right. As had been true for the astronauts' flights to the moon, the critical legislative "window" was open and in the right position in 1967—as it had not been before and might not be later—for the public television proposal.

The final bill, as introduced by Senator Magnuson on March 2, 1967, embodied the recommendations contained in the Carnegie Commission and the president's message. In Title II, the authorization for CPB specified that it would *not* be an agency or establishment of the federal government and that its board would be composed of fifteen members, appointed by the president for six-year terms with the consent of the Senate. The consent requirement had not been proposed by the commission, nor had it recommended presidential appointment for more than 6 of the 12 members it proposed.

Five weeks after the bill was introduced, the Senate Subcommittee on Communications opened hearings. At the start of the hearings on April 11, 1967, Senator John Pastore, chairman of the subcommittee, keynoted the bill with this statement: "The opportunity before the Congress and the challenge of this issue are of paramount importance for the future growth of this nation. It is an opportunity and a challenge that may be forever lost if we turn our backs against the proposals outlined in this legislation. It is my hope that this legislation may be enacted by the Congress of the United States during this session."

And indeed it was enacted. The legislation passed through that time window and reached the President's desk for signature on November 7, 1967. The full course from introduction to signature had been run in slightly over eight months. This was almost a record congressional run for controversial, innovative, federal action in the sensitive area of the media. The passage had been expedited primarily by the high priority given it by a legislation-conscious White House, which was supported by the prestige of the Carnegie Commission and the commitment and professional skill in HEW. The educational television community, through a second national conference, achieved an uncharacteristic unanimity expressed in expert opinion at legislative hearings and in lobbying visits to congressional offices.

But that speed of passage should never be interpreted as evidence of unrestricted support for the concept of federal involvement in broadcasting. Although it was not directly expressed, there was Republican and southern Democratic concern, particularly in the House of Representatives, that this step might lead to federally controlled telecasts or to a propaganda channel for the incumbent administration. The federal aid to education hurdle had been cleared two years earlier, but fear about the possibility of federal strings on local instructional ventures in broadcasting was still prevalant. A reflection of this legislative apprehension can be observed in a number of amendments. The proposed corporation was prohibited from owning or operating broadcasting facilities. cpb was mandated to provide interconnection, but it was barred from creating a network which would lessen the independence of the stations or would impose, without station participation, a nationally determined broadcast schedule. These barriers were raised to place distance between federal funding and actual decisions to air programs.

The most persistent anxiety, however, focused on the so-called public affairs programs, those broadcasts which dealt in a journalistic fashion with controversial issues. In the view of some uncertain supporters, it was necessary to ban political activity by the corporation and to prohibit the editorial from the public air. In a significant move to guard against corporation support of advocacy journalism, statutory language was inserted by the House to require "objectivity and balance" in all programs relating to controversial issues. These prohibitory amendments gave sufficient assurance to reluctant House members so that a majority vote for passage was achieved. But, as will be described later, these amendments created complications in system development and pointed toward governmental instrusion in program decisions.

At an elaborate signing ceremony at the White House —with congressional leaders, broadcasters, and their supporters in attendance—President Johnson completed the legislative course that resulted in the Public Broadcasting Act of 1967 and signaled the way toward implementation in these words:

... and most important—it [the law] builds a new institution; the Corporation for Public Broadcasting.

This corporation will assist stations and producers who aim for the best in broadcasting; good music, exciting plays, and broadcasting reports on the whole fascinating range of human activity. It will try to prove that what educates can also be exciting.

It will get part of its support from our government. But it will be carefully guarded from government or from party control. It will be free, and it will be independent—and it will belong to all the people.

Television is still a young invention. But we have learned already that it has immense—even revolutionary—power to change, to change our lives.

I hope that those who lead the corporation will direct that power toward the great and not the trivial purposes.

At its best, public television would help make our nation a replica of the old Greek marketplace, where public affairs took place in view of all the citizens.

But in weak or even in irresponsible hands, it could generate controversy without understanding; it could mislead as well as teach; it could appeal to passions rather than to reason.

If public television is to fulfill our hopes, then the corporation must be representative, it must be responsible—and it must be long on enlightened leadership.

CPB'S FIRST BOARD OF DIRECTORS

This new law was to be translated into action in what then became *public* broadcasting (radio had been added to the scope of the corporation by congressional amendment) by a presidentially selected board of fifteen. The qualifications for such a board were listed in the statute as a guide to the president:

(2) The members of the board (A) shall be selected from among citizens of the United States (not regular full-time employees of the United States) who are eminent in such fields as education, cultural and civic affairs, or the arts, including radio and television; (B) shall be selected so as to provide as nearly as practicable a broad representation of various regions of the country, various professions and occupations, and various kinds of talent and experience appropriate to the functions and responsibilities of the corporation.

The momentum that had been generated by congressional action could hopefully be sustained by early designation of the board. However, only two directors were named—James Killian, the chairman of the Carnegie Commission, and Milton Eisenhower, president of Johns Hopkins University—at the time of the signing. The stature of those nominations emphasized President Johnson's desire to have outstanding and respected national figures assume the sensitive leadership responsibility of CPB. But more than three months passed before the balance of the slate and the selection of Frank Pace, Jr., former budget director and secretary of the army, as chairman were announced. The delay was indicative of other demands on the president's time as 1967 passed into 1968 and the Vietnam war entered the phase of the Tet offensive. But it probably was also a sign of some second thoughts and uncertainty about the role and position of this new institution. The media and the academic community had increased the volume of their protest against the conduct of the war. Would this extension of the media with federal backing add new sights and sounds of opposition?

These doubts were probably magnified by the appearance of the Public Broadcasting Laboratory (PBL) in that same season. This new entity in the ETV system was another Ford Foundation venture to advance the cause of national programming. Fred Friendly, after his resignation from CBS in 1966, over the network decision to preempt a broadcast of Senate foreign policy hearings in favor of a situation comedy rerun, had become television advisor to the foundation's new president, McGeorge Bundy. Friendly was convinced that a major TV undertaking of an innovative nature, with an adequate budget, delivered in prime time to all ETV stations, would attract national support for the public medium. The initial programs played to mixed reviews, after a massive advertising campaign that heralded a TV miracle. The journalism was professional and tough and, as would be expected, critical of presidential decisions. The title, Public Broadcasting Laboratory, was confused with the label for the new corporation, and its product was attributed to that embryo organization.

The complete slate of directors of CPB included a mixture of professional backgrounds and met the political requirement that no more than eight of fifteen members were to be from one party. The directors were confirmed by the Senate after a brief hearing before Senator Pastore's subcommittee. There was minor complaint in the industry that the board members possessed little direct experience in ETV, except for Frank Schooley, who was the manager of the TV and radio stations at the University of Illinois. Critics at NET observed that the CPB board membership was hardly as distinguished as its own. But the elements of the system shared the sense of achievement in the presence of the CPB board and began to anticipate the impact of the expected federal funds.

While the board proceeded with its incorporation of CPB as a nonprofit institution in the District of Columbia, the search was conducted for a chief executive officer. The quest stretched out over several months while Chairman Pace gathered a small staff to commence studies of action required under the act. Finally the search committee of John D. Rockefeller III, Oveta Culp Hobby, and Milton Eisenhower turned to me, in the waning days of the Johnson administration following the Nixon election. I responded affirmatively, the board approved the selection, and I assumed office as CPB president in February of 1969, fifteen months after the passage of the act that established the corporation and in the first month of the new Nixon Administration. In retrospect, and without any tendency toward retroactive self-flagellation, this selection suffered from three liabilities. First, even though my service in the Kennedy–Johnson administrations had been in the nonpartisan area of civil service, my presence was viewed by some as evidence of Democratic influence. Second, my long-time federal service was judged to be a forecast of governmental behavior on the part of CPB and contributed to the perception that CPB was in fact an agency of the government. Third, I had had no direct experience in broadcasting, commercial or educational, in my career. These liabilities complicated the acceptance of the corporation's leadership by the elements in the system. It is for others to identify any offsetting assets that may have justified the selection.

COMMUNITY SERVICE GRANTS

In early decisions, the CPB directed its attention to four areas of system development. The first of these was the community service grants to the independent stations to assist in their growth as a public service instrument to the citizens within reach of their signals. From the outset the board confirmed the station as the essential element within the system. CPB funds should be provided to permit the station to extend or enrich its broadcast service in accordance with its own determination of needs and priorities. The only exclusion related to plant and equipment, which were already susceptible to federal assistance through the facilities program administered separately by HEW. The proportion of total CPB appropriations to be devoted to station grants was a continuing point of debate with the station managers. Naturally, the station management was eager to gain an ever larger share of the corporation's appropriation for unrestricted support of local operations. As the appropriation level rose and more resources were expected, this pressure for growth became more intensive. Likewise, the formula for distribution among the highly diversified units was constantly studied and reevaluated by CPB in concert with the managers. All parties recognized from the start that CPB contributions to station operating funds were additive and were intended to attract more local support, public and private, rather than replace any portion of that support.

The first distribution in 1969 was a flat ten thousand dollars to each station, thereby avoiding differential judgments until later. The following year and through 1972 the amounts were computed on the basis of relative expenditure levels of the stations, with a rising minimum for the smallest and a rising maximum for the largest as the CPB appropriations increased. A more complex and equitable formula was developed with stations in 1972. That formula gave more recognition to the size of the audience served. The range of differences among the stations proved a stumbling block in the design of a totally fair system.

ESTABLISHMENT OF THE INTERCONNECTION

Second, CPB focused on the establishment of the mandated interconnection of the stations by telephone lines to permit live, instantaneous service to all stations and to construct an economic delivery system for national programs to the expanding range of stations. An interconnection had been temporarily arranged for PBL on a two-hours-a-week basis, and occasionally NET would contract for one-time use of long distance telephone lines to deliver a special program to stations; for example, an extended discussion by journalists and experts on a presidential state of the union message. But the corporation considered its mandate to be for a full-time service to link the stations for both national and regional program distribution.

A limited and temporary arrangement was negotiated with AT&T for initial service in 1969, with the understanding that a comprehensive and full-time system would follow. The statute permitted the provision of this service "at free or reduced rates" by the carrier. This permission, with its ambiguity, necessitated representation by CPB for free service. This request was rejected by AT&T, and the FCC supported the rejection. When continued AT&T–CPB negotiations failed to arrive at an acceptable charge, the FCC adopted a short-term incremental cost standard which produced a rate about 30 percent of the commercial rate for the interconnection system specified by CPB. This meant that the basic delivery system would cost five million dollars annually. In view of the corporation's inability to pay at that level, FCC and AT&T accepted a plan for incremental payments of one million dollars a year until the five million dollar level was reached.

The technical requirements of the system called for construction that delayed completion of the interconnection for all specified points until 1972. During the interim, national programs without topicality were taped and distributed by mail to the unconnected stations.

This distribution pattern served all stations without charge. Each station was able to receive programs for immediate transmission, for taping and later transmission, or for no use at all. The flexibility of station programming was thereby greatly enhanced. The existence of this physical capability made possible closed circuit communication as well as circulation of programs for station review in advance of distribution time. In this fashion the technical means for a national system were brought into being, with benefits in enlarged program resources and capability.

PROVISION OF NATIONAL PROGRAMS

The third area of system development, provision of national programs of "excellence and diversity," was responsive to the major purpose behind the act. CPB could not produce such programs itself; ownership of facilities was prohibited. Instead, the acquisition of programming was to be accomplished through grants to or purchase from program production sources within the system—NET or the individual stations. There was no exclusion of outside sources, such as commercial TV or film producers, but, with funds very limited relative to program costs, investment within public broadcasting was desirable if quality and variety could be assured.

CPB funds would supplement those granted by the Ford

Foundation, which continued to be the principal financier for national programs until 1971. From its earliest days, CPB consulted with the foundation, as well as with station representatives, in order to complement its program support. From the first, joint CPB–Ford Foundation support was standard practice for the principal national offerings. In addition, and with increasing success, the corporation and the producing stations sought program underwriting from other foundations and from the corporate world.

The decisions in this area were bound to draw fire. Interests and tastes differ. There were never sufficient funds to permit the desired breadth and diversity or to undertake ambitious new program concepts. Selection of producers created problems for those selected and envy for those not selected. All elements of the system sought participation in these decisions, even though the corporation had statutory responsibility and financial accountability. But I return to this critical area in the next chapter, in which the product of the system will be treated in the detail it deserves.

A VARIETY OF SUPPORT ACTIVITIES

The fourth area of system development, system support activities for CPB to perform, was listed in the act. Unfortunately, the stations gave these activities low priority. Nevertheless, small amounts of money were allotted to these purposes. A nationwide information system was designed and installed in CPB to collect and store basic data about stations, their facilities, organization, key staff, and finance. This information was used in planning and decision making. Grants were authorized to facilitate staff training and to enlarge minority opportunities. Staff assistance was offered to stations for local fund raising, program promotion, and community service. The corporation accepted the responsiblity for an annual conference of station managers and later for more frequent sessions to discuss current issues on a regional basis. Some of these services were carried out in collaboration with NAEB, the professional association of the industry, others through ad hoc arrangements with the stations.

When CPB moved to secure the interconnection, it was evident that future management and utilization for that system asset was a source of concern to the stations. When NET and PBL had employed the interconnection for distribution of national programs in the previous year without the involvement of the station managers, that had caused tension. To lessen this tension, CPB immediately agreed to collaborate with a group of managers, selected by the ETS/NAEB and the NET Affiliates Council, in the design of an organizational mechanism. In a series of meetings this six-member committee collaborated in the design of a station-oriented agency to manage the interconnection, represent the stations in national program selection, coordinate, and schedule those programs produced for distribution. This pattern was very different from that of the commercial networks. It placed in the hands of the user station delegated responsibility in the national phase of the system.

THE FORMATION OF THE PUBLIC BROADCASTING SERVICE

This separate organization, designated Public Broadcasting Service (PBS), was to be governed by a board of directors consisting of a majority of station representatives plus public members and the presidents of CPB and NET. As a nonprofit corporation, it would function in accordance with District of Columbia law and would receive its total financial input from CPB. The goals, structure, and relationships were defined by CPB with the committee, whose organizations agreed to the design at the NAEB convention in November 1969. Before that assemblage adjourned, the first board members had been selected. Within ninety days the veteran manager of WGBH in Boston—Hartford Gunn—accepted the presidency, and PBS set up shop in Washington to prepare for the first national season to open in October 1970. Another set of initials was added to the system roster. The day-to-day decisions and operations were placed another step away from the government and closer to the local licensee. A completely unique although complicated and delicate structure, with meaningful station involvement, had been created with almost total acceptance by all parties concerned.

Those parties had differing perceptions of CPB's position in the structure. Frequently referred to as "one of the funding agencies" by some program producers, CPB was perceived to be a federally-funded Ford Foundation. These producers believed that it should engage in benign grantsmanship. It should divide and distribute its federal pie with few questions to PBS, producers, regions, and stations. On the other hand, some board members and government spokesmen assumed that the corporation was lodged at the peak of a pyramidal structure from whence commands could be issued to the rest of the system. Both extremes were in error, but the truth in between was so complex and delicate that misunderstanding was a high probability. The balance of relationship had to be maintained in equilibrium through constant communication, goodwill, and confidence among the elements.

Although the corporation had statutory power, it could not command. Although it had responsibility for system leadership, it could not move forward without the consent of the other elements. Although it was authorized to speak for this new enterprise, it was not the only voice to be heard, and it had no assurance that the other voices would sing the same song.

Under these system conditions, the vulnerability of the enterprise to internal tension and disharmony and to external confusion and misunderstanding was quickly revealed. That vulnerability was a constant companion of those who were determined to create and sustain the means for irrigating the wasteland. Their endeavors to plant the program seeds and to pump the financial waters are chronicled in the following two chapters.

II

To Create and Deliver a Message for the Public Good

All too frequently McLuhan's claim that the medium is the message has been valid in public broadcasting. The overpowering concern about structure, relationships, and technical means has preempted the basic purpose of the system: to provide programs to the citizen viewer, programs which will educate, enlighten, and entertain.

The system designers' objective has been to shape an environment in which creative forces can find expression in the images that appear on the home screen. This objective can be easily subverted in a rigid or instable system, just as it can be frustrated by conflicts in direction and taste. The multiplicity and instability of the system elements during the first years of public broadcasting placed a hardship on program production. The artistic and journalistic successes were frequently achieved in spite of rather than because of the system conditions. Political and financial tensions within the system tended to be heightened through program crises.

Public broadcasting was intended to be a supplementary or alternate service that did not duplicate commercial offerings. But more important, public broadcasting has a special concern for the public's interests and needs. Although all TV licensees are committed to public service and are expected by the FCC to ascertain public needs in arranging their program schedules, the noncommercial, educational, or public station has a magnified obligation to meet these standards.

Virtually all public stations had been established to serve the educational community. The medium was to be employed in the classroom, where it could bring new instructional assistance to the teacher. School systems arranged with the stations for telecasts in foreign languages, scientific principles, music, and art—any academic discipline susceptible to visual presentation. In the early days these programs were largely of local design and tended to be the camera's view of the classroom. Some teachers who were successful in the classroom were unable to teach through the new media. The small box with its picture was of limited value in class if the picture was only another teacher performing in the same manner as the live teacher.

School administrators had perhaps hoped that use of this technological device would decrease instructional costs. Such savings were rarely realized. TV production costs were high. When low-cost productions were attempted, they failed to enrich the student's understanding. After all, that student was spending more time before his home screen than he did in school, and he was fully aware of the most professional television that commercial sponsors could buy. And the teacher who believed that television would decrease educational costs by reducing the total number of teachers was not overjoyed at the presence of this video competitor seated in his class.

NEVER A NATIONAL CURRICULUM

To reduce costs and raise quality, collective means of program production were developed with and for the station—but with the understanding that this would not result in any kind of national curriculum. Local TV material might be produced elsewhere, as text books are, but the ultimate decisions about use would remain with the school system. In fact, the broadcaster, in many jurisdictions, had little to say about the programs he transmitted during school hours. When he produced a program in his own studio or in the community with his mobile unit, he functioned as a job shop for the local educators.

The cooperative ventures were centered in regional networks supported by member stations. In the northeast, EEN developed significant interstation participation in new programs which met a common educational need throughout the region. The National Instructional Television Center (NIT) was created at Bloomington, Indiana, with a start-up grant from the Office of Education, to serve local and state broadcasters with common needs. In Nebraska, the Great Plains Center offered a catalog of videotapes for use by broadcasters and teachers in organizing their video curriculum. Small fees, usually less than local production costs, were charged for use of these materials.

TALKING FACES

It became fashionable to criticize the quality of this service to education as little more than "talking faces" and of marginal benefit to education. Teachers and administrators became restive with the time inflexibility of broadcasts in the classroom and with material that placed the teachers in a secondary role. It is true that the high expectations were not realized, but the product did improve in content and sophistication. Imaginative educators extended the use to more and more subjects in some parts of the country, particularly in the south. More and more the unique visual qualities in television were used to illustrate concepts and conditions that could not be presented in more traditional classroom modes.

Major attention was given to subjects at the elementary levels, but again particular combinations of broadcasters and teachers moved up the academic ladder to secondary, collegiate, and adult levels. The current spreading interest in nontraditional study has properly restimulated the original support for media-delivered instruction. The inclusion of television in England's new Open University— the massive approach to provide higher education to those adults previously unable to enter the university—has conferred academic respectability on the home tube. In almost every state, there is a project in process to develop an American copy or adaptation of this model. In its report, the Commission on Nontraditional Study, under the chairmanship of a former educator–broadcaster, Samuel Gould, identifies a lengthy roster of external degree programs, campuses without walls, and other departures from the traditional modes of post-secondary education. Many of these experiments have components calling for television, but only as a supplementary—and not the exclusive —educational means. Where television has successfully met learning needs, there are no professors on screen, but there is academic participation in the professional research preparatory to program production. This area of technology has contributed new approaches to learning when such collaboration exists. The final product is sufficiently flexible in format and high in visual quality to satisfy the teacher's

needs or—where the learner is outside the school walls—
to attract and hold his interest.

THE IMPERATIVE OF COMMUNITY SERVICES

Before recounting the system-wide struggles with educational technology, the noninstructional sector of the
local program scene should be examined. The amount and
quality of locally developed programming have depended
on funds, equipment, and talent. Many a station manager
with a tight budget originates only an hour or two of programs each week. I recall visiting some stations where
studio space remained dark because the resources could
not be secured to use it, and stations whose service was
limited to one or two locally originated programs each
week. Many stations preferred to use mobile units, which
carried the camera to the personality or event, rather than
staging programs at the stations. Even the modest CPB
community service grants opened new program gates.
For the first time, a station could cover local government
in action, could start a consumer assistance series, could
offer a forum for a local election campaign, could provide
a showcase for community music and drama, or could encourage expert dialogue on critical issues. In several cities,
with assistance from the Ford Foundation or other underwriting, stations attempted journalistic experiments in reporting local developments. This trend was accelerated by
KQEDs successful "Newsroom," which began during San
Francisco's newspaper strike.

This category of program received less critical attention
than the national production. But by 1970 it constituted
27 percent of the total six hundred thousand hours of programs transmitted by all public stations. The impact of
this service on the community cannot be measured by ex-

isting research techniques. Examples, cited in cpbs 1971 annual report, help to illustrate what was undertaken by individual stations in response to community needs.

Lubbock, Texas. When one thinks of urbanization, the city of Lubbock, Texas, does not fly to mind. Yet Lubbock, like communities everywhere, increasingly finds that it must come to grips with new problems caused by burgeoning growth. KTXT-TV, the public station associated with Texas Tech University, did something about it. The station produced seventeen hours of incisive programs called "People and Problems." Installments in the series dealt with such topics as "Crime, Criminals, and Cops," "Traffic, an Endless Highway," and "Help Wanted." The programs involved almost every local official and civic leader, and the public, too—citizens sent in questions or appeared in person to ask them. Hardly had this series ended when nature took a hand in adding to Lubbock's problems. A tornado ripped through the town, destroying almost a quarter of it. KTXT-TV responded again, this time with "The Road Back," a five-part series that focused on rebuilding and preparation for future disaster.

Richmond, Virginia. In Virginia, the General Assembly meets once every two years, and some of its most important business is conducted during its closing hours. wcve-tv, Richmond, embarked on a "first" in the state; it telecast, live, the final ten hours of the session, running from 7 P.M. to 5 A.M. An editorial in the *Norfolk Virginia Pilot* commented on "most viewers' startled reaction: Is that what goes on in Richmond?" Largely as a result of the coverage, a new campaign was begun to streamline the procedures of the legislature. The coverage prompted Governor Linwood Holton to join with the state's lieutenant governor and the Speaker of the House in a statement citing the program as "public television's finest hour in the state." wcve also broadcasts in their entirety (and up to fourteen hours, on one occasion) the weekly Richmond city council meetings. When it appeared that those broadcasts would cease because of lack of station funds, money was donated by the community. "Thus," commented *TV Guide*, "the people of Richmond ably demonstrated by their concern—and dollars—that rather than let this experiment go down the drain, they would work and give to have democracy in action brought to them, every Monday night at 7 P.M., right in their living rooms." In such coverage, WCVE hardly stands alone in public television. The number of stations that broadcast meetings of governmental bodies—state, county, and local—is growing and includes such dispersed stations as WETA in Washington, D.C., WEDH in Hartford, Connecticut, KUON in Lincoln, Nebraska, WGTV in Athens, Georgia, WTVI in Charlotte, North Carolina, KOAP in Portland, Oregon, WVIZ in Cleveland, Ohio, and WJCT in Jacksonville, Florida.

Jacksonville, Florida. Through feedback techniques, in fact, wjct has become an integral link between citizens and government in Jacksonville and has improved responsiveness at both ends. While such meetings take place, the station opens its lines to citizen comment, and this comment has frequently affected official action. For its work in providing an on-air rumor control center during disturbances, WJCT was also credited with lessening civic tensions.

San Diego, California. KPBS, San Diego, provides another example of initiative. When a series of scandals rocked the city government in early 1970, the station became convinced that only part of the problem had surfaced. So it plunged into two months of investigation which culminated in a special report, "City on Trial." As a result of new information brought out in the report, a grand jury probe was renewed and the station won widespread citizen acclaim.

Los Angeles, California. KCET, Los Angeles, exhibited community concern by providing what was probably public television's longest "special" of the year; gavel-to-gavel coverage of the inquest into the death of Reuben Salazar, well-known Mexican–American reporter and broadcaster. The coverage lasted almost seventy hours and was credited with giving the Chicano community an opportunity to voice concerns and frustrations that might otherwise have boiled over.

These are some of the ways in which public broadcasting covered and, in some cases, made news. But the real life of any community proceeds in quieter ways that seldom make the headlines. And in these areas, stations responded, too.

State of Maine. On one end of the age spectrum, Maine Public Broadcasting presented a weekly series for senior citizens called "A Time to Live" that covered everything from stamp collecting as a worthwhile hobby to the high cost of prescription drugs.

Dallas, Texas. Children are the concern of "All you Need is Love," a series from KERA, Dallas, through which prospective parents can "meet" children who are available for adoption. In the early months of the program, the program succeeded in finding homes for more than thirty children.

Chicago, Illinois. "Day Care Today and Tomorrow" was the title of a special from WTTW, Chicago, that examined the shortage of such facilities. Following the program, and in part as a result of it, the mayor established a new city agency to facilitate day-care center development.

Austin, Texas. Children are the beneficiaries, too, of "Carrascolendas," from KLRN, Austin. The program is like other children's shows in all ways, except that it is conducted in Spanish and English, with the goal of removing the language barrier that faces Chicano youngsters.

State of South Carolina. "Job Man Caravan" from the South Carolina ETV Commission tours that state, providing information about jobs and training for the unemployed and underemployed.

THE TURNED ON CRISIS IN PITTSBURGH

To stimulate local initiative for this type of programming, in 1971 CPB inaugurated annual awards for community service. The first such award was presented to WQED in Pittsburgh for its remarkable series on drug abuse— "Turned On Crisis." This endeavor started as a purely local effort by the station. As the project's success in Pittsburgh was demonstrated, it became a national feature, with support not only from CPB but from private foundations and corporations and from the federal government through the National Institute of Mental Health (NIMH). It was a major national program, distributed by PBS for its schedule, along with localized information on the drug abuse crisis.

A key ingredient in making this drug education series meaningful was the decision, made early in the planning stage, to involve citizens from the many communities in the Pittsburgh area. This required WQED to initiate and activate groups of people and organizations that could undertake the leadership in a series of "Mini-Town Meetings." The "Mini-Town Meetings" brought interested citizens together to view the televised program prepared by the station and then to voice their opinions on what could be done about the drug problem in their community. After contact was made with groups in a total of twenty-nine communities in western Pennsylvania, WQED proceeded with a concentrated on-the-air campaign that lasted the entire month of October. The schedule involved showing the initial weekly program each Sunday evening, with a repeat on Tuesday evening. "Mini-Town Meetings" were held on Sunday, Monday, Tuesday, and Wednesday of each week. Then, on Thursday of each week, a televised "Town Meeting" was held at WQED's studio, with participants drawn from representatives of each of the "Mini-Town Meetings." The station, however, sought more than a series of conversations at these meetings. Rather, it sought community commitment and action. Months after this concentrated campaign, twenty-two of the twenty-nine communities continued meetings and continued to seek solutions to the drug problem. While WQED's evening prime-time attention to the subject was being aired on Channel 13, its sister public TV station, WQEX, Channel 16, broadcast a series of television programs dealing with various aspects of drug abuse and related social problems Monday through Friday from 6 P.M. to 1:30 A.M. This "Electronic Bibliography" of over one hundred hours of films and videotapes was gathered from sources all over the country. The combined effort via the two channels provided a unique opportunity for parents, educators, and civic groups to gain knowledge of the drug problem via the medium of television.

To insure maximum participation, WQED conducted a total promotional campaign. News releases, on-the-air promotional announcements, radio spots, billboards, bus and taxi cards, a month of daily newspaper ads, and special mailings to schools and other interested groups flooded the Pittsburgh area. In addition, special kits were provided for community groups and schools. These included a drug fact book, meeting guides, audiovisual and printed bibliographies on drugs, posters, flyers, buttons, a drug glossary, a discussion leader's handbook, and other informational material. The reaction of citizens of Pittsburgh to "The Turned On Crisis" was summed up in an editorial in the Pittsburgh *Post-Gazette* on March 11, 1970. Said the paper:

Few projects in the history of public television are more relevant to the times than the series of nightly programs on drug abuse launched this week by Station WQED.... Thoughtful viewers of "The Turned On Crisis" series ... may achieve fresh insights into a social question which directly or indirectly involves them. The WQED team which undertook the organization of a vast diversity of material deserves the gratitude of a community it has labored to enlighten.

The possibilities for significant and imaginative community service are infinite. They are restricted only by the absence of resources, funds, talent, and equipment. Local station management and the national system developers must work together to overcome these restrictions. This goal, however, should be more clearly defined. It should not be an emotional or political plea for local autonomy without a serious program justification. What community needs can best be met by television? How can the medium most effectively reflect the unique human qualities of each community? How can it serve to communicate the community's attainments and its changes, its values and its problems? How can television provide representativeness for all elements in the community through involvement and access? How can it serve as an informational source for the learner, consumer, and taxpayer without becoming an editorial instrument of government? How can it preserve freedom of inquiry and opinion when supported in large measure by public revenues? These questions must be answered through assessment of local needs, design of program to meet those needs, and continuing critique of program effectiveness.

The existence of federal funds in greater volume to supplement local support can produce an essential difference. But the station leadership must plan for, and must justify in community service terms, the employment of those funds. The garden plots already planted in the local wasteland give abundant testimony to the potential benefit. With planning based on community need, these plots can be expanded and blended with the national service produced elsewhere in the system and shared through the interconnection.

THE MIRACLE OF SESAME STREET

Education, community service, television artistry, research, and promotion were all beautifully blended to conjure up that amazing place, "Sesame Street." That miraculous program, designed to educate through entertainment the more than twelve million preschoolers, was and is public television's supreme success. Its appearance on the screen, in November 1969, revolutionized the prospects for educational broadcasting, children's programming generally, and public television especially. "Sesame Street" was cited so frequently in support of federal funds for public broadcasting that one congressman stopped my glowing testimonial one day in 1971 with, "I know 'Sesame Street' is great, but what else have you done!"

At the time of the Bay of Pigs, President Kennedy remarked that the Chinese had taught him that "success has a thousand fathers, failure is an orphan." "Sesame Street" has a thousand fathers; CPB was only one in that throng. The almost simultaneous arrival of the new organization and the new program on the television scene was an undesigned piece of mutual good fortune. The arrival of CPB resulted in limited, and later substantial, financial support for the program. But more important, the CPB-provided *interconnection* permitted national distribution of the program to all public stations. "Sesame Street" was a perfect vehicle for the new system. It attracted more than half of the target audience—as much as 90 percent in certain prime target areas like Bedford-Stuyvesant in Brooklyn —and it lured adults and older children to the public channel. Urged on by their viewers, stations repeated each program two, three, and even four times (a late showing was arranged in northern Indiana to teach English to adults in ethnic communities). Stations quickly assembled the week's programs and ran them back to back throughout the Saturday morning hours when commercial stations showed cartoons. Several corporations contributed funds to cover the cost of this upgrading in weekend viewing for children. Yes, PBS became the "Sesame Street" network at the time of its inception.

How did the system have the genius to produce "Sesame Street"? It didn't. The concept for the program was developed by Joan Ganz Cooney, an experienced broadcaster, and shaped by Lloyd Morrisette, a foundation executive with commitment to educational innovation, and by educational advisors and television producers. From the outset the goal was high quality, which needed high financing. The investment had to be massive, but it was protected by preproduction research and planning, by top talent in direction, production, and performance, by community promotion and utilization efforts, and by postproduction research and evaluation. The big gambler was the federal government. Harold Howe, the commissioner of education in 1968, was captured by the proposal and its potential and provided five million dollars. The remaining three million dollars came from the foundations and, in 1969, from CPB.

To produce this series of 150 one-hour programs, a new organization was formed—the Children's Television Workshop (CTW). Originally an independent unit within NET, after the first year's success CTW was made a separate, nonprofit corporation. More than eighteen months were devoted to the preshowing stages of the project. The educational purpose was to teach numbers, letters, and concepts to children during their peak learning period and when they were already viewing television many hours each day. Clearly these purposes could be met in the classroom, but these children were at home. The necessity to work through the curriculum selection process of thousands of school systems was avoided. Success was measured by contrasting the learning levels in these cognitive skills of those who did and those who did not watch the programs. Eventually many schools included the program in their instruction, and the rapid progress of learning for the Sesame generation prompted more advanced instruction in kindergarten and first grade.

CTW's acclaim was reflected not only in countless awards for educational and broadcasting excellence but also in continued support for "Sesame Street" and other projects. With a new emphasis on improved reading capacity, CTW moved forward with a successor program in that area. Employing the production techniques of "Sesame Street," this new series, "The Electric Company," was designed to assist the early reader, ages six to nine, to understand word meanings, letter groupings, and sentence structure. The learning was surrounded by the entertainment that delighted viewers of that age group. Some of their favorite TV actors showed up to help with the reading—most notably Bill Cosby, who was concurrently pursuing a degree in education at the University of Massachusetts between television appearances.

Yet another CTW project is in the planning stage. It is a series intended to deal with family health issues. This theme recognizes that the American citizen's concern about his health is second only to his worry about income, and so it is relevant and should attract many viewers. The project represents an ideal program objective in terms of public broadcasting purposes of service to the citizen and his family.

MORE FOR CHILDREN

Programming for children, both at home and at school, was a prime objective of CPB from the outset. Commercial programs for children were for the most part far out in the wasteland. Mothers were organizing to protest commercial children's programs and their particularly aggressive advertising appeals. A national commission investigating violence placed a searchlight on children's fare. Perhaps there were those who viewed this program area as universally appealing and free from political controversy, but the demand for constructive children's viewing was high, inside and outside of the system.

Prior to the advent of CPB, the stations had clamored for NET to provide, through its tape distribution service, more children's programs. With their funds already committed to cultural and public affairs programs, NET agreed to supply a Pittsburgh-produced series, "Misteroger's Neighborhood," to stations at one hundred dollars per week. Since other programs provided at no cost to the stations were considered by many to be less desirable, this arrangement requiring local payment for a highly desired program irritated many station managers. Starting in 1970, CPB was able to finance this program's production and interconnection distribution without charge to the stations. Fred Rogers, the one-man genius of this neighborhood, brought a gentle, sensitive, and individualized message to young children through his mixture of reality and make-believe. Joined by "Sesame Street" and "The Electric Company," this program completed the two hours of children's programs each weekday starting in 1971. In response to a later station demand, PBS repeated delivery on Saturday morning over the full-time dedicated interconnection. The repeat lessened station taping and transmission cost on that extra day.

THE MIDDLE-AGED CHILDREN

Within the system there was still a call for a weekly program that would involve what one of the dying issues of *Life* magazine labeled as the middle-aged children— those from seven to thirteen years of age. All stations were urged by CPB and PBS to seek new and attractive program formats for that special audience. The result was "Zoom," a show written and performed by seven lively boys and girls of that age group who were assembled and guided by an understanding producer at WGBH in Boston. Scheduled by PBS in the early Sunday evening hours, "Zoom" has set records with family audiences. A measure of its success was the receipt of 193,887 fan letters in the first six months on the air. These fans contributed riddles, games, pieces of film, and drawings, many of which became program substance on following Sundays. The refreshing antics of these free-spirited and talented volunteers proved the value of originality in television production and the capability existing within the public broadcasting system to achieve that originality.

HAIL TO THE BBC

In the arts, national program development was a natural line for the public broadcasting system to follow in filling the cultural gaps left by the mass audience programs from the commercial networks. Except for occasional specials of distinction, the 1973 CBS Shakespearean play, and the 1968 NBC Heifitz concert, the commercial schedules offered an entertainment diet of mysteries, situation comedies, and movies. The theatrical productions of the early days of TV have diminished to a limited few. The advertising imperatives forced commercial producers to play the rating game with intensity. The weekly program rankings were the box scores for the network executives. Low ranking forecast short life, no matter what the artistic merit of the program might be. Public broadcasting did not have to live by these imperatives. In its quest for diversity, it sought not a mass audience but the many different audiences of age, taste, and interest. Although it obviously did not wish to go unseen, it could recognize that a cultural program viewed by the relatively small TV audience of three or four million was exceeding the capacity of theatre or concert hall by a factor of many thousands.

If "Sesame Street" was public television's most appreciated gift to the children of the nation, the dramas from the British Broadcasting Corporation were the top success with the adult fans of drama, literature, and history. The prominence of these British imports in the PBS schedule prompted critics to brand public television as "BBC's rerun house" or to urge tourists to visit London for advance viewing of later public television features.

The BBC had been a valued program source for NET productions prior to the interconnection. Under the NET arrangement with the Ford Foundation, 50 percent of NET's production was to be in the cultural area; the other half was to be in public affairs. The availability of dramatic material from the BBC permitted low-cost, high-quality acquisition for that area. With that objective in mind, in 1969 the NET international procurers picked up the remarkably successful BBC series dramatizing Galsworthy's endless novel, "The Forsyte Saga." In a direct purchase from the BBC, NET acquired the rights to distribute the twenty-six episodes to public stations for transmission over a three-year period at a bargain price in TV program terms. In subsequent acquisitions from BBC the price rose, not only because of the audience acclaim given this series but because the producers' increased interest in Yankee dollars resulted in the designation of a United States sales agent, *Time-Life*.

The Forsytes became a familiar sight on public channels, starting during the first interconnected season in 1969–1970. Although some of us gagged at its advance billing as a "British Victorian soap opera," the excellent writing, acting, and production justified its appeal to the largest adult audiences attracted up to that time. Each episode was distributed twice a week, many stations added one or two additional showings, and complete second and third distributions were provided in later years. In the ultimate gesture of addiction, WNET in New York ran all episodes consecutively in a 24 hour period for particularly hardy fans and those who missed an episode during earlier runs. The "Saga" was no competitor in the ratings, but Susan Hampshire won an Emmy for her portrayal of Fleur, a newly published run of the books enjoyed high sales, and *The New Yorker* indulged in Forsyte cartoons.

"MASTERPIECE THEATER"

The BBC trend was sustained in the subsequent conception of the "Masterpiece Theatre." The process by which that program matured was a demonstration of the multifaceted system in program design. Whereas NET had captured the "Saga," WGBH in Boston opened the negotiations for the acquisition, adaptation, and financing of a continuing series of BBC dramas. With support from CPB and PBS, the Bostonians worked out a plan whereby the station producers would select from the BBC drama treasury a series which could constitute a broad cross section of literature and history. The number of programs in each series would vary, but approximately thirty one-hour episodes would be acquired. To give the entire series a continuing frame, WGBH would produce an opening and closing commentary with a distinguished personality; they were able to sign their first choice, Alistair Cooke, a British journalist with long-time American associations. The entire program package was then presented to a number of corporations for possible underwriting. Mobil Oil was interested and eventually covered the cost of acquisition, the adaptation production, and the public promotion—an amount which came to nearly half a million dollars each year. In consultation with PBS, the interconnection schedule was designed to deliver the first showing of each program on Sunday night, followed by a second distribution later in the week.

The programs were enthusiastically received by the stations and the media critics, with the "Henry VIII" and "Elizabeth" series in 1971 setting a new peak of audience interest. The performers were awarded top recognition in competition with all other TV performers. The commercial networks were not oblivious to this rising curve, and the BBC-Time-Life combination was able to sell the two series for commercial use, thereby demonstrating another principle of public broadcasting: the provision of quality programming will influence subsequent commercial program selections and thereby expand the audience impact of such programming. This same principle was evident in the drastic improvement of sponsored children's programs following the high acceptance of "Sesame Street."

"CIVILISATION" ON TV

No account of BBC contributions to American public broadcasting can conclude without mention of Kenneth Clark's "Civilisation" series. As soon as that highly publicized visual tour of western civilization's monuments appeared in Britain, it was identified as ideal for the new national schedule on PBS. But the BBC preferred the larger audience and higher prices of the commercial networks until those broadcast avenues were closed. Ultimately an acquisition was negotiated by NET, and the series was distributed in prime time to widespread critical acclaim and extensive viewer interest—as indicated by the best seller status of Clark's fifteen dollar book of the series' words and pictures.

The success of Clark's venture prompted internal demand for a series on American civilization as a possible video centerpiece in the bicentennial year, 1976. It was concluded with regret that the existing capacity for program production within public broadcasting was insufficient for a project of such magnitude. Preliminary exploration of the concept by a reputable independent producer generated cost and time estimates beyond the system's resources and created negative political waves within the system. The program goal was blessed but deferred. With more than a touch of irony, the BBC called upon its correspondent, Alistair Cook, to undertake such an American series. When it was completed, the series was sold to a commercial network for viewing by the American audience.

DOMESTIC TV DRAMA

Not all drama was imported. A decided effort was directed toward domestic production, but here the limited resources were, again, a serious handicap. American viewers have been exposed to the BBC standard of quality, and the system could not afford to offer second-rate material; comparable projects could well run in excess of one hundred thousand dollars an hour. But several production centers were encouraged to apply their own resources in dramatic productions. An ambitious venture called Hollywood Television Theater was launched at KCET in Los Angeles, under the experienced direction of Lewis Freedman. Play scripts were adapted to the visual assets of television. Professional actors of the first rank performed for modest payment. The casts were kept small and the production settings simple. The results were most heartening. Several productions revealed the special strength of television in dramatic presentation. One play in particular, "The Andersonville Trial," received widespread honors and was repeated again and again in response to audience request. The ultimate expectation was the formation of a well-funded continuing center for the regular production of TV dramas.

At WQED in Pittsburgh, a different technique called "docudrama" was employed for system-wide display. From a current or historical happening—for example, campus disorders in the 1960s or the Boston massacre trial in the 1770s—a drama was written and produced. The format gave new meaning to the event through the dramatic interpretation of the actions and emotions of the men and women involved in the events.

The drama capability of NET was continued after it was

organically merged with the New York public station in 1970, to combine national and local production in a single organization with facilities for broadcasting as well as production. That capability had special strength in the operatic art. Under Peter Herman Adler, three seasons of WNET opera were produced. Not merely aiming the camera at the opera stage, these productions of both new and traditional works were restaged to take full musical and dramatic advantage of the medium's flexibility. They were unfortunately flawed because of the serious inadequacies of sound reproduction in currently manufactured receivers. In an experiment to overcome this deficiency, the sound was broadcast on FM stereo radio where public radio stations existed in the same receiving area as the television station. This was highly successful and proved the value of the interplay of the two media as well as the need for improvement in the audio capability of television sets.

FROM ROCK TO BACH AND BACK TO JAZZ

Diversity was emphasized in the arts and to a high degree in music. In that first summer of 1969 a Sunday night musical series, with Steve Allen as anchor man, was produced by NET. In its thirteen programs the series ranged the full sweep of musical taste, from Pablo Casals to Arlo Guthrie and from the Marlboro Festival to the New Orleans Jazz Festival. The very diversity in the performing arts brought cultural programming out from under the safe and noncontroversial shelter. Few viewers complained about the Boston Pops, but the more frenetic music of the counter-culture and the symbolism of avant garde dance caused ripples of dissent in some quarters. When, in 1972, a modern ballet number purported to display nudity, critical reviewers and legislators objected vehemently to the use of public funds for such displays—even though the performance was hailed for its aesthetic merits. Some contemporary lyrics or poetry were permeated with language of the street, and some stations refused to transmit or attempted to blip offensive language. Such action by stations was accompanied by howls about censorship from producers and station grumbles about excessive New York influence in program selection.

This situation stimulated action within the system to develop program standards—and a process for application of those standards—that would be fair to producer, distributor, and transmitter, but particularly to the citizen-viewer. In that audience there existed pluralism of interest with varying levels of taste. The programs were available to them in their homes at the turn of the dial, a viewing condition quite different from the paid visit to theater or gallery. The issue remains one of preserving freedom of choice over a broad range of options without offending taste or mores of particular portions of the audience. With government funding underlying the issue, new and special implications of freedom and responsibility are injected into the program decision process. Even if that injection is not specified, it is present in the perception of those who produce and those who transmit. That perception may lead to self-censorship or to defiant challenge.

WHAT IS PUBLIC AFFAIRS?

The most serious program zone of combat, however, was in the territory of public affairs. The term itself was misleading and misunderstood. I prefer to describe this zone as video journalism in the broadest interpretation of that term: from straight news coverage, to expert analysis of events, actions, or trends, to televised hearings or debates, to documentary treatment of current issues, to interviews with leading personalities, to participative involvement of citizens. It is the video newspaper, magazine, textbook, lecture, and governmental coverage. Because of its power to report in visual terms, television can give the citizen a new dimension of understanding about the world in which he lives.

Video journalism, with this power to illuminate vital issues, has failed in both public and commercial sectors to gain the strength, reach, or diversity commensurate with its potential. On the commercial channels its freedom to range the field of public problems is inhibited these days by the commercial imperatives of broadcasting and by a barrage of ambiguous threats from public officials. Less and less time is devoted by broadcasters to the exposition and discussion of the critical problems that face Americans everywhere. More and more caution is applied in dealing with those few problems that are presented. At the same time the public is telling the pollsters that television has become its principal source of information and that, contrary to the allegations of public officials, a significant majority believes that what they receive is "fair and balanced in showing different points of view."

Commercial networks continue to invest large sums of money in their news departments. CBS spends over fifty million dollars annually to sustain CBS news. The evening and morning news coverage by commercial networks is expert but brief. Occasional analyses are packed into such short time periods and interrupted so frequently by commercials that viewer comprehension is limited. Treatment of major events—the presidential inaugural, space shots, and natural disasters—continues to give the public a sense of historic participation through his home viewing. But investigative reporting, though at infrequent times penetrating and hard hitting, is sporadic and less daring. The pursuit of diverse views on controversial subjects is mild and limited. What efforts are attempted tend to set new lows in the rating competition and experience difficulty in attracting the sponsor's dollar.

If these economic hurdles were not high enough, the commercial news director has been forced to face new obstacles erected for him by the vice president and other assorted White House spokesmen. These obstacles take the form of personal attacks on the objectivity of broadcast correspondents, the proposal for local station policing of network journalism, and the threat of antitrust suits against alleged collusion among liberal commentators. Critics can scarcely condemn broadcasters for displaying lack of eagerness in extending their journalistic efforts over an obstacle course with such official hazards. The victim of these adverse conditions is the citizen who turns on his set to expand his own knowledge of the issues.

But what about video journalism in *public* television? With an even more fundamental obligation for public service, the noncommercial stations have an inherent mandate to inform their viewers. Without the economic and time stresses of commercial broadcasting, journalism on the public station should treat public issues in depth and breadth. There should be opportunities for experimentation with new techniques and formats that more fully employ the versatility of the medium. Education for citizenship through presentation and discussion of current controversies should be a basic objective of public television.

When the first educational stations were licensed, each sought in its own way to deal with the public issues of interest to its viewers; each endeavored to create its own video journal. Limited technical and professional capacity permitted only partial performance. To overcome this deficiency, a number of stations formed the cooperative regional networks, sought funds from the Ford Foundation in support of local newsrooms, and appealed for a national service which could offer the desired topicality and professionalism. These moves were modestly successful because of the generosity and understanding of the Ford Foundation in its support of local newsrooms and of NET and PBL public affairs programming. Although these supportive actions were greeted with heckling as well as applause from the benefiting stations, they demonstrated the supplementary journalistic role that educational television could play.

"THE SOCIAL DILEMMA AND THE POLITICAL PICKLE"

When the Carnegie Commission invented "public" broadcasting in 1966, it clearly encompassed video journalism in that institution. The commission in its report urged that the opportunity "is at hand to turn the instrument [TV] to the best uses of American society and to make it of new and increased service to the general public." Essayist E. B. White, in an almost poetic expression of that opportunity, wrote in the same report that noncommercial television "should be our Lyceum, our Chautauqua, our Minsky's and our Camelot. It should restate and clarify the social dilemma and the political pickle."

Much of the commission's debate centered around the need for adequate insulation of this type of programming from the potential interference of that public sponsor, the United States government. To achieve insulation, the commission coupled the establishment of CPB with a long-range financing plan immune from the pressures inherent in annual appropriations.

When the president and Congress acted in 1967, they deferred that long-range financing feature. The promised action to provide that second step has been postponed from year to year in the intervening period. It is more distant than ever today following the presidential veto of even a modest congressional move in that direction last year.

THAT FOB FACTOR

At the time the original bill was being considered in the House of Representatives, the qualms about bias and imbalance in journalistic programming were impediments to passage. Congressman William Springer gained added support for the bill with an amendment that incorporated congressional intent in statutory language of an explicit nature:

(g)(1)(A)...facilitate the full development of educational broadcasting in which programs of high quality, obtained from diverse sources, will be made available to noncommercial educational television and radio stations, with strict adherence to *objectivity* and *balance* in all programs or series of programs of a controversial nature. (Emphasis added.)

So objectivity and balance were joined to the already present standard of fairness to coin public broadcasting's fairness, objectivity, and balance (FOB) factor.

These flashing lights of caution were visible when the infant corporation contemplated the journalism component of national programming to be backed with federal funds. There was whispered advice to avoid all controversy inherent in such programming for at least five years or until long range financing was a reality. "Limit your funding to symphonies and children's programs—play it safe" was the gratuitous counsel offered. But public broadcasting would have failed in its public service mission if it had turned its camera away from the stormy landscape of controversy over vital issues.

Through the creation of PBS and the assignment of funds to independent production centers for journalism projects, the corporation endeavored to remove editorial judgment from the source of funds. It was intended that CPB become a heat shield against political fire that might be generated in the form of outside criticism of specific programs. CPB would determine, after receiving PBS and station advice, the need for a particular type of program, the capability of a particular station to produce it, and the availability of funds to finance it. But the production center, working with PBS, would develop program content, create the format, select the talent, and produce the program for national distribution through the interconnection. The station manager would still serve as the final editorial point, however, when he decided whether, when, and how many times the program—the final product— would be transmitted to his viewers. This complex of relationships creates a delicate balance of responsibilities. The decision making was in fact shared and built on an assumption of mutual confidence. The system of fragile checks and balances was essential in view of the sensitivity of the government–journalist relationship in the influential and highly exposed environment of television.

With the new federal funds to supplement past Ford Foundation initiatives, creative ideas and new production sources were encouraged and explored. That target of unpopularity, the effete northeast, was no longer the exclusive source of documentaries and public service programs.

To strengthen the professional journalism base in Washington, the National Public Affairs Center for Television (NPACT) was formed by the leadership of WETA (the local station in the nation's capital), augmented by national directors from business, labor, journalism, law, and education. This center assumed responsibility for Washington-originated or related projects for national distribution. There was no news coverage as such. That was properly left in the commercial domain. Issues and trends were discussed in a weekly round table of top Washington journalists and in one-to-one interviews by the political reporter of the *Atlantic Monthly*, Elizabeth Drew. With the advent of the political year 1972, two experienced broadcast journalists, Sander Vanocur and Robert McNeil, were hired by NPACT to develop and present video accounts of the presidential campaign from the citizen's point of view. In addition, these correspondents moderated live and taped coverage of hearings and presidential speeches and arranged for expert reaction and analyses after such events. Although NPACT is based in Washington, many of these programs were prepared in other locations around the country and engaged reporters from other public stations for local or regional news.

The line-up of public affairs programs included various sources and approaches to public affairs. From San Francisco came a weekly program—"World Press"—in which foreign press was analyzed by experts. From Boston and Los Angeles came the novel "Advocates" program, in which a courtroom setting provided well-developed arguments in support of and in opposition to precisely stated public issues that faced early decision. Viewers were urged to consider both arguments and then make their own decisions and advise their elected representatives and the "Advocates." On some issues responses flowed in from ten and even twenty thousand citizens.

From New York came Black Journal, a direct communication with the Black audience, designed and performed by Black production teams. From South Carolina and across the country came William Buckley and his "Firing Line," which was added to the national program roster in response to station requests for an articulate moderator with a conservative philosophy.

From around the country in 1972 and produced out of New York came "Bill Moyers' Journal," in which the former newspaper publisher discussed with Americans the issues and problems of their concern. And from the same New York source came documentaries and an innovative video feature called "The Great American Dream Machine," which employed satire as a means of commentary about the passing scene.

Documentaries and satire struck sensitive nerves. Some individual programs, limited in number in relation to the total inventory, are well remembered for the controversy they evoked:

Castro's Cuba, a sympathetic treatment of the Cuban leader by a visiting camera crew;

Who Invited Us?, a condemnatory thesis on United States intervention abroad, which omitted World War II;

The Banks and the Poor, a critical video essay that described bankers' treatment of the disadvantaged and included inferences of conflict of interest involving congressmen with bank board membership;

FBI Subsidy of Violence, an investigative piece—in the Great American Dream Machine—which was deleted from national distribution and then broadcast anyway after the producing station transmitted it;
The Woody Allen political message which was withdrawn by the producer before broadcast.

These five and a few others brought closer examination to this type of program. Liberal journalists perceived the difficulty to be government pressure on a weak CPB. Conservative critics claimed that CPB failed to exercise adequate control over program decisions. And neutrals questioned the quality and fairness of the journalism and the ability of a government-financed system to permit press freedom.

SYSTEM-DEVELOPED STANDARDS OF JOURNALISM

These experiences within the system exacerbated the relationships between PBS and the producing centers, particularly in New York, and between producers and stations. But demands for greater editorial control by the stations or by PBS or CPB were redirected toward the formulation of standards and processes for video journalism by the system itself, PBS, stations, and producers. With PBS in the lead, this action involved the expert advice of journalists from inside and outside the sysem. The following broad standards, developed through this self-disciplined approach, became the foundation; more detailed guidance spelled out how the standards might be observed:

we recognize the obligation to be fair;
we pledge to strive for balanced programming;
we recognize the obligation to strive for objectivity;
we acknowledge the obligation not to let technique become the master of substance;

71

we recognize the obligation to reflect voices both inside and outside society's existing consensus.

To implement these intentions, in 1972 PBS appointed James Lehrer—the anchor man of the Newsroom at KERA, Dallas—as public affairs coordinator; a twelve-member public affairs panel was designated "to advise the PBS staff concerning judgments in handling public affairs programs"; and each producing agency was urged to prepare "its internal manual of guidelines for journalistic production." In April 1972, the CPB board formally accepted and commended these actions and reaffirmed its previous support of public affairs programming.

VIDEO JOURNALISM—30 PERCENT OF NATIONAL PROGRAMS

It was eventually concluded that programs in this area should constitute about 30 percent of the national program time distributed to the stations by PBS. The other 70 percent would be composed of cultural, children's, and general educational programs. The 30 percent proportion was supported by the majority of the stations which transmitted these programs upon receipt or shortly thereafter. A small but vocal minority considered this, or any percentage, excessive and, in a very few instances, some programs or series were not transmitted at all.

That FOB factor, reinforced by the journalistic standards, was always engraved in large letters high on the wall even when there was no reminder of its presence by its authors. The desired balance in programming, both within series and in the total schedule, was purposefully pursued through the addition of new reporters or panelists with differing views, through live or taped coverage of events not carried on commercial television, and through the pro and con exposition of issues on the "Advocates."

Nevertheless, the new personalities who were associated with previous political positions—William Buckley, Bill Moyers, and Sander Vanocur—drew criticism despite their current performance in accordance with the standards.

The system's complexity was revealed by the complaints that reached CPB about the presence of Martin Agronsky, a veteran TV and radio newsman, on public television. The stations on Eastern Educational Network (EEN), seeking a nightly news program—which national distribution did not provide—contracted with Agronsky to produce and lead such a program for distribution to EEN stations at 10 P.M. Those who considered Agronsky too liberal and anti-administration were incredulous over CPB's absence of control. But CPB was in fact not involved in this decision. The stations established the program need, selected the reporter, and financed both production and distribution. Their own circuits remained after CPB activated the national interconnection. They were totally self-sufficient. They were able to contract for a service that they wanted with a journalist they liked, and they paid for it with their own funds.

PRIME TARGET: VANOCUR

Vanocur, however, became the prime target. His alleged close association with the Kennedys and some of his public statements about presidential press relations gave him a low popularity position at critical power centers. Even those who acknowledged his professional capacity would not believe that his on-air performance could be truly objective. His appointment attracted additional attacks when it was revealed, in answer to a congressional inquiry, that NPACT would pay him $85,000 a year—exactly twice the annual sum received by congressmen. This revelation triggered further inquiries about salaries in public broadcasting, and in the 1972 legislative process it generated moves to place limits on salaries through statutory restrictions.

The delicacy of the structure for program decision making and the balance in the program schedule itself were subject to stress and strain. Some subjects, editorial judgments, issue interpretations, and personnel selections sparked protesting observations from special interests, station representatives, and government spokesmen. Within the system, disputes of this type sustained intramural rivalries and undermined collective progress. Bitter and accusatory letters were exchanged between station managers and producers. Favored press representatives were courted by the opposing parties. Devil theories on individual motivations were circulated. Although these episodes were infrequent, when they did occur they reflected the uncertainty and frustrations remaining within the system. Moves toward corrective action were perceived as responses to official objections and as evidence of federal control over the system by CPB. *Variety* converted the corporation's initials to the Corporation for Patsy Broadcasting. On the other side, those who opposed public broadcasting or its involvement in journalism considered their own opposition substantiated by these disputes.

The Nixon administration's dissenting position on the system's development was openly presented in the speech by Clay Whitehead (director of the Office of Telecommunications Policy) to the NAEB convention in Miami in October 1971. His broadside attack was not entirely unexpected, but it was more intensely political and more in line with other administration attacks on the media than might have been expected. The charges were designed to shake that uneasy structure by condemning the alleged centralization of CPB and PBS while wooing the stations through the cry for more financial recognition at the "bedrock of localism." The principal trigger for that barrage was the journalism included in the national program. The content and personalities had displeased executive leadership, which was fully aware of television's potency—so aware that the prospect of supporting potentially critical coverage of administration actions with federal funds was distinctly unattractive.

Whitehead's view of video journalism was elaborated in a radio interview on New York's station WBAI several weeks after his Miami blast:

> There is a real question as to whether public television, particularly the national federally funded part of public television, should be carrying public affairs, news commentary, and that kind of thing, for several reasons. One is the fact that the commercial networks, by and large, do quite a good job in that area. Public television is designed to be an alternative to provide programming that isn't available on commercial television. So you could raise the legitimate question as to should there be as much public affairs, as much news and news commentary, as they plan to do.... When you're talking about using federal funds to support a journalism activity it's always going to be the subject of scrutiny. The Congress will always be watching it closely. It just invites a lot of political attention.

An earlier warning along these lines had been sounded in less militant tones by FCC Chairman Dean Burch, in September 1970. He pointed out that "Congress seems to call upon public broadcasting to be fairer than fair." He appealed for the behavior of Caesar's wife and urged the hiring of some noncreative conservatives if it was indeed true that all creative staff members were liberals.

But the threat of interference was brandished by the executive and not the Congress. Objections to programs were infrequent from Capitol Hill until the administration opened its attack. While deploring the alleged centralized control in CPB and PBS, the administration representatives applied pressure on the same organizations behind the scenes to exercise more control over video journalism. These demands were more openly directed in late 1972, after the president's veto of the CPB authorization bill and the addition of six more Nixon-appointed or reappointed board members. In recent public statements, serious doubts have been raised about the continued CPB funding of any but a select few of the public affairs programs. Already the stations' involvement in the program selection, scheduling, and coordination has been curtailed through the elimination of PBS in these functions. The full responsibility for these functions has been directly assumed by CPB—a much greater and tighter mode of centralization.[1] The distance between funding and program decision has been sharply contracted. The heat shield has been penetrated. The likelihood of editorial control from the government has been decidedly heightened. The criticized centralization appears to be an admired reality.

[1] The reduced scope of PBS activities and the assumption of broader CPB involvement in program decisions produced a state of civil war in public broadcasting during the spring months of 1973. A reconstituted PBS, with active leadership from station board chairmen, resisted the CPB moves which had been prompted by the administration. CPB was forced to withdraw from this position described above, after protracted negotiations with PBS during which alleged pressure from the White House resulted in the resignation of the new CPB board chairman, Thomas Curtis. His successor, the Carnegie Commission chairman, James Killian, was able to restore the earlier relationship in an agreement with PBS concluded in June. The escalating Watergate attention, particularly the Senate hearings, which were carried in prime time on public television, diverted administration concern about this issue.

These recent developments raise serious questions about future federal funding of video journalism. The perception of control following the granting of funds has been confirmed. The possibility of a government news network is too high a price to pay for federal support. Freedom must be maintained in providing this essential public service to the viewer. Alternate modes of financing must be sought to preserve that freedom, even if the rate of system development must sustain delay and uncertainty for even longer.

In education, children's and family programs, culture and the arts, and video journalism, a pattern of diverse programs has been produced and distributed to enrich the inventory of offerings available to the more than two hundred transmitters. To pursue the wasteland analogy, small but promising plots have been staked out, and seeded, the nourishment from a moderate increase in funding and facilities has improved the scene and attracted viewers, the greater visibility has evoked a variety of responses, and the benefits of even more extensive cultivation have been demonstrated while the system problems in achieving that cultivation have been identified and only partially solved.

Now is the time to turn to the financing urgencies and options and to the means for achieving program excellence and diversity. Recognizing the program that the viewer receives on his screen as the fundamental purpose of this delicate and fragile system, in what ways can revenues be secured to build strongly, creatively, and freely?

III

To Finance Television Without Commercials

Television is a high-cost enterprise. No discounts or economy sizes are available just because it is programmed in the public interest. Perhaps that worthy purpose gains extra contributions in time and talent, equipment and cash. But this flow of *pro bono* generosity has never been sufficient to fulfill the aspirations and potentials of public television. In large measure the system-building endeavors of the past few years have been aimed at national patterns and mutual assistance to tap those financial resources that can raise this service to a viable level. This fund search has been both the unifying force that caused the disparate elements to establish and seek common goals and the divisive friction that has disrupted the course of development. The failure to achieve stable, massive, and long-term revenues from a variety of sources has retarded the growth of program services of high quality, innovative content, and broad diversity.

Yet these realistic points of assessment, with their dreary relation of prospect to achievement, fail to acknowledge progressive financial trends which have at least moved toward expectation even if they have fallen short or lagged behind the flowering vision of the system advocates. What are the financial dimensions in the system picture? What are the spending levels and the income totals? What are those dollar trend lines? What have these conflicting and unifying tendencies really produced? What degree of citizen, institutional, and governmental commitment has been demonstrated and might be developed into expanded future support? These and other related questions lead the hunt for answers in this third safari into the vast wasteland.

There is a natural inclination to concentrate on the national financial successes and failures because they have been played out in the well-lit arena of executive and congressional behavior. That is where the high stakes are. That is where the Carnegie Corporation and the Public Broadcasting Act of 1967 promoted the concept of federal supplementary support from that magic but illusive resource: assured and insulated long-range financing. That is where the sensitivities of government–medium relations can be dramatized on the stage of Washington politics. But this is only a small segment of the picture.

FINANCING FROM THE LOCAL LEVEL

In each of the two hundred communities where the station transmitters are located, the financial meaning is immediate in terms of plant and equipment, hours on the air, local program production, instructional assistance to the schools, or facets of community service. It is the perpetual concern of the station board and manager, who must meet payrolls and purchase equipment and supplies. To them the national campaign is largely to ease that concern through direct grants, national programs through the interconnection, and reinforcing supplementary services. The climb toward self-sufficiency is engineered differently in each situation with steps provided by state or local tax revenue, contributed services from commercial broadcasters, foundation grants, corporate contributions, on-air auctions, and viewer subscriptions.

But there is a total system. Since CPB constructed a system-wide information collection and analysis process, financial data has been available to permit that total view. The last full year for which such data has been published is the fiscal year ending June 30, 1971. Fragmentary data for the following twelve months can be cited to update some trends.

THE STATION FINANCIAL PICTURE

To start with, there were 207 stations operated by 133 licensees in fiscal year 1971. These two figures are necessary because licensees in state systems and in some large metropolitan areas operate more than one station or transmitter. Since 1971, the climbing birthrate has produced a total of 227 stations and 137 licensees—a rate of about one new station per month. These numbers should be subdivided:

Category	Licensees		Stations	
	Number	*Percent*	*Number*	*Percent*
Universities	44	(33)	61	(29)
School Systems	22	(17)	23	(11)
State Authorities	21	(16)	67	(32)
Community	46	(35)	56	(27)
Total	133	(100)	207	(100)

SOURCE: Financial Statistics of Public Television Licensees, Fiscal Year 1971, National Center for Educational Statistics and Corporation for Public Broadcasting.

Total income for all licensees, from all sources, was *$141 million* that year, up 41 percent, from $100 million the previous year. Direct operating costs came to *$113* *million,* up 35 percent, and capital expenditures were *$29 million,* up 43 percent in a year's time.

The income total of $141 million can be tracked back to ten basic sources in these amounts and percentages of the total:

Source	Amount (in millions of dollars)	Percent
(1) Federal government Primarily the educational television facilities program administered by HEW	8.9	6.3
(2) Public broadcasting agencies Almost exclusively CPB community service and program production grants	14.8	10.5
(3) Universities Primarily publicly supported institutions	9.6	6.5
(4) Local school boards and local governments	21.0	14.2
(5) State boards of education and state governments	46.4	33.0
(6) Foundations Overwhelmingly the grants of the Ford Foundation	15.8	11.3
(7) Business and industry contributions	3.0	2.2
(8) Auctions	3.8	2.8
(9) Subscribers and individuals	8.4	6.0
(10) All other sources	9.7	6.9

SOURCE: Financial Statistics of Public Television Licensees, Fiscal Year 1971, National Center for Educational Statistics and Corporation for Public Broadcasting.

AN UPWARD ADVANCE

The comparison with 1970 levels reveals an irregular pattern of growth. Each source staged an advance with the exception of local schools and government, which showed slippage—1.4 percent for schools and 13.1 percent for government. The plus side sported increases of 92.9 percent for federal funding, 80.2 percent from CPB, 86.9 percent from foundations, and 86.4 percent from state government.

The tax support categories—federal, state, and local, including universities—provided 72.5 percent of the total income. So only about a quarter of the support came from truly voluntary sources. Although these sources of funds had been expanded by dint of effort and expense, their percentage of the total fell off in the two-year period.

In tracking federal fund influence, there was an evident tendency in terms of budget for the smaller licensee to receive a larger share of its total from federal funds. The high budget stations were more likely to build support from foundations, contributors, and state government.

The total of $113 million for operating expenditures was broken down as follows:

Budget item	Amount (in millions of dollars)	Percent of total	Percent increase
(1) Technical	25.7	22.7	+20.5
(2) Programming	17.4	15.3	+28.2
(3) Production	32.7	28.8	+76.3
(4) Instruction	8.8	7.7	+28.1
(5) Fund raising	4.1	3.6	+31.1
(6) Promotion	3.0	2.7	+33.4
(7) Personnel development	.2	0.2	+10.1
(8) General administration	15.7	13.8	+24.0
(9) All other operating	5.8	5.2	+12.2
Total	113.4	100.0	+35.5

SOURCE: Financial Statistics of Public Television Licensees, Fiscal Year 1971, National Center for Educational Statistics and Corporation for Public Broadcasting.

Costs were on the rise across the board. Heavier expenditures for technical and production needs, lighter outlays for instruction and programming, and high expenditures for fund raising in terms of funds actually raised—these conditions are apparent from the figures.

RISING CAPITAL EXPENDITURES

On the capital front, total payments rose to nearly $30 million in 1971, bringing the accumulated capital expenditures to *$212 million* since that first station took to the air eighteen years before. This capital pie was sliced to meet a variety of needs: land acquisition, 7.7 percent; buildings, 1.2 percent; antenna systems, 8.6 percent; transmitters, 11.8 percent; microwave equipment, 4.0 percent; control room equipment, 7.9 percent; video tape recorders, 9.8 percent; TV cameras, 8.3 percent; all other equipment needs, 20.7 percent. The volume of capital expenditures has paralleled the volume of annual operating expenditures; the larger the licensee's budget, the larger the total capital expenditures to date. Community and state licensees have accumulated the largest amounts over time ($78 million and $62 million respectively). The *median* station plant value is *$1.6 million*, with state licensees' median higher at $2.4 million. The vast spread in station plant is impressively indicated in a high total at $10.2 million and a low at only $16.8 thousand, hardly in the same league in broadcasting capacity.

This spread is also reflected in an analysis of comparative operating budgets for the licensees. This budgetary range extended from a high of $17 million to an incredible low of $36 thousand, a range greater than the population difference between California and Alaska. If the median level for each of the four types of licensees is examined, the range is reduced, but the differing conditions are still impressive:

Category	Amount
University	$ 318,000
School System	$ 370,000
State	$1,079,000
Community	$ 551,000

SOURCE: Financial Statistics of Public Television Licensees, Fiscal Year 1971, National Center for Educational Statistics and Corporation for Public Broadcasting.

The high–low spread persists in each group. Even the community stations go from a low budget of $47 thousand to that high of $17 million.

The distribution of licensees in some budgetary dollar ranges provides a picture of the financial configuration of the enterprise and the basis for the station community service grants from CPB from 1970 to 1972:

Range	Number of licensees	Median
Under $100,000	8	$ 58,129
$100,000 to 249,999	18	$ 154,286
$250,000 to 699,999	60	$ 374,640
$700,000 to 1,999,999	35	$ 969,735
$2,000,000 and over	12	$2,996,576

SOURCE: Financial Statistics of Public Television Licensees, Fiscal Year 1971, National Center for Educational Statistics and Corporation for Public Broadcasting.

THE CPB FINANCIAL ROLE

For fiscal year 1971, CPB reports its own resources available and applied at *$31.6 million*. It received a congressional appropriation of $23 million, which was supplemented by other federal grants and contracts ($711 thousand) and nonfederal contributions ($5.1 million: foundations and corporations, 70 percent from the Ford Foundation, interest and carryover from the previous year). This represented an increase of $12.6 million over 1970; the appropriated amount had risen $8 million from the $15 million that traversed the full process the year before. The pattern for appropriations had changed as well as the amount. The authorization act for the two years, 1971 and 1972, introduced the concept of incentive matching. The appropriation consequently had two parts: a definite amount, in this case $20 million, and an additional payment to match up to $3 million in nonfederal funds. The volume of nonfederal funds exceeded this figure in response to the incentive and to permit the maximum of $23 million.

Out of the available resources, CPB made grants and awards totaling $24.6 million, an increase of $14.3 million over the prior year. The balance of nearly $6 million was applied to programs administered by CPB, administrative support, and carryover for the next year. Out of those grants, CPB invested just under $10 million for national television programs or local sequels to such programs, such as "The Turned On Crisis." PBS received $8.4 million for the interconnection, program coordination, scheduling, and promotion, including the payment of $2 million to AT&T for the long lines. The balance of the TV funds were paid out to the local stations in community service grants to station licensees and regional networks in accordance with budget levels specified earlier, from a low of $12,500 for the smallest to $32,500 for the largest. These amounts were supplemented through competitive production grants for program proposals that might ultimately be available for what the Carnegie Corporation called "more than local" use. This contribution to station growth came to $4.2 million that year, or about 18 percent of the television money (the balance of grants found their way to radio stations).

This distribution demonstrated the policy decision to establish the interconnection service and to augment national programs as the most important and highest priority action with the limited funds available. It was reasoned that these investments would benefit the stations by enabling them to produce improved and diverse programs that would attract an enlarged audience and thus increase financial contributions. At the same time CPB would provide modest and initial supplements to local sources of support. This judgment was later disputed by station leaders—particularly those who differed with program and producer choices—and by administration spokesmen, when they claimed that local development had been deprived while a national network and national program schedule was constructed.

The mainpoint of station criticism, however, was the level of CPB funding. The original expectation, after the act was passed in 1967, was that long range financing would arrive shortly and that presidents and Congress would honor the Carnegie Commission objective of $200 million of federal support within a five-year period or by 1972. The history of those five years dashed these lofty expectations. The Congress only provided seed money of $5 million that first fiscal year of 1969. That came so late, in October 1968, that the board inaugurated a minimum of planning operations with funds pledged by CBS and the Carnegie Corporation. Both organizations came forward with $1 million at the time of the presidential signing. This pledge of private support was intended to prove that

CPB would, in fact, benefit from both private and public funds.

Before a second year's federal action could start, there was the change in administrations without even a preliminary public move toward the promised long-range financing. The departing Johnson administration forwarded authorization and budget requests for $20 million—a fourfold increase, but hardly the long stride toward $200 million. In its budget review upon taking office, the new Nixon administration cut the request back to $10 million; a doubling of the first year was considered a fair and prudent lift until the new administration could thoroughly evaluate this strange creature inherited from its predecessors.

Congressional attitude was generally supportive of the higher figure. In the Senate hearing on the authorization bill, Senator Magnuson commented that the amount was too small and that "the Pentagon dribbled away that much every day." In the House, leaders such as Congressmen Torbert Macdonald and William Springer were concerned over the absence of any long-range financing proposal and warned that this might be the last year the House would accept a single-year authorization. Thus Congress maintained pressure on the administration to present such a plan at the earliest date. The substantive content of such a plan was not even suggested by these congressional spokesmen.

A bill authorizing the compromise figure of $15 million for fiscal year 1970 was finally passed, and the administration supported that amount in the appropriation process, which culminated in providing the $15 million. This was applauded as a three-fold increase, but it was scarcely a fast incremental climb toward the Carnegie goal.

SHORT STEPS TOWARD LONG-RANGE FINANCING

The long-range financing approach was a dominant preoccupation within CPB. At its bimonthly meetings, the board always devoted time to discussion of this matter. The management staff sifted existing research, pushed new studies, discussed possible approaches with administration budget representatives, and raised the topic at every meeting they had with station managers and their organizations. By the summer of 1969, an Advisory Committee of National Organizations (ACNO) was formed by CPB to secure citizen input. This advisory Committee was to be a broad spectrum of national public interest groups who would advise CPB on all matters relating to public broadcasting, but particularly with respect to its ultimate financing. Comprised of representatives from groups ranging from the PTA to the American Bar Association to the AFL–CIO to the National Council of Churches—more than thirty in all, the advisory committee met quarterly, with CPB staff, to review proposed programs, react to the current offerings, and give evidence on the condition of citizen interest and support.

Concurrently a group known as the National Friends of Public Broadcasting was formed by Mrs. William Schuman, a volunteer leader at the New York station. This group was to give mutual assistance to volunteers active in citizen support work in all of the stations. Although the group's members, drawn ultimately from at least one hundred stations, concentrated on local efforts to raise funds, promote viewer activity, and assist station managers, they too gave outside backing for moves toward long-range financing.

The first financing proposal, designed for application starting in fiscal year 1971, was prepared by CPB in the first few months of its existence in 1969. This plan combined the Carnegie Commission recommendation for a manufacturers' excise tax (2 percent rising to 5 percent) on the sale of television sets with a fund matching device where federal funds would be authorized to match nonfederal funds entering the total system on a one dollar for two dollars basis. A legislative package with these provisions was actually circulated in the executive branch by the Bureau of the Budget in May 1969. Although the corporation never officially reviewed the accumulated comments from the interested executive agencies, it was advised that its proposal failed to receive the desired administration backing. The Treasury Department and the Bureau of the Budget have a natural aversion to dedicated taxes in any administration, and in this type of clearance procedure their position was expected to be negative on that feature of the plan. The submission of the proposal was intended to raise the issue for policy consideration in the administration before the next round on an authorization bill. An alternate and interim approach for financing was forthcoming from the administration early in 1970, in the form of a *three-year* authorization with open-ended dollar amounts and provision for a matching of CPB nonfederal income up to a specified limit.

These conditions were discussed in congressional hearings on the authorization bill in 1970. The hearings were, for the most part, productive of affirmative results. No specific problems were raised by members of Congress.

Congressional attitude, except for that of long-time experts and advocates, was more apathetic than supportive or hostile. Where there was knowledge of the system, there was an affirmative response. FCC Chairman Dean Burch and Education Commissioner Sidney Marland gave positive administration backing. President Nixon's education message in March pointed to television and educational technology as desired areas for educational improvement. Pressure for long-range financing was tempered by the interim plan and by evidence of general support.

HELP FROM THE COMMERCIAL SIDE

Senator Pastore recognized the difficulty faced by CPB in attempting to raise the matching maximum of $5 million from nonfederal sources, and he encouraged the management to seek contributions from commercial broadcasters. This suggestion had already been acted upon. Following the earlier lead from CBS, NBC made a grant of four hundred thousand dollars, spread over four years, to CPB, and additional capital grants totaling a million dollars to stations in cities where the network owned and operated stations. Except for this support, solicitation visits with other networks and groups of commercial broadcasters along the line of Pastore's suggestion were unavailing. These fund-raising calls unfortunately coincided with the broadcasters' loss of cigarette advertising and a general decrease in advertising revenues. The resulting discussions did reveal, however, that many commercial stations were contributing equipment and service to local public stations. One broadcast group, Westinghouse, opened the way for even closer collaboration between its stations and the neighboring public station and offered its program library for possible national distribution to the public system.

Throughout this early CPB period, close and beneficial communication was maintained with commercial broadcasters through regular meetings with network presidents, speeches at gatherings of broadcast executives, discussion with officials of the National Association of Broadcasters (NAB), and more detailed exchange of views with a special committee established by NAB for this purpose. At the 1970 hearings and in later legislative rounds, testimony was offered by the NAB and the network presidents urging passage of the interim measure and early action on long-range planning.

THE ANCHOR MAN AND THE CABINET LADY

With the 1970 bill en route to passage, public broadcasting experienced a situation that revealed the political sensivity of the system. After the House hearings were concluded but before the bill was reported out of committee, the Washington newspapers carried a report that William Westendieck, the anchor man of the "Newsroom" program at WETA, the local public station, had been fired because his wife had become press secretary to the wife of Attorney General John Mitchell. The program and its anchor man had only been on-air for two weeks, hardly an adequate time to judge his performance, and media sensitive political leaders interpreted the dismissal as political action by the station management. Because the concept of the newsroom program was a favorite with the Ford Foundation, which was providing the major part of the financial support of this Washington venture, there were suggestions of political interference by the foundation. To air the controversy and set the record straight, Chairman Macdonald reopened his hearings before the subcommittee and called all parties to testify on the case. It was established that the station management had acted without external pressure but had probably overreacted to the anchor man's familial connections with the controversial cabinet lady. The program continued for another eighteen months under several different anchor men and was terminated because of lack of sufficient funds and absence of demonstrable viewer demand. But the escalation of this episode to a subcommittee hearing and White House inquiry indicated political vulnerability. For many months there was speculation around the system about the impact of this case on the level of the funds in the authorization bill.

THE LIFT OF A TWO-YEAR AUTHORIZATION

A two-year authorization bill was passed. It represented a compromise of the three-year version approved by the Senate and the one-year version approved by the House. A maximum fund level of $30 million was set along with an additional $5 million if matched by an equivalent amount in CPB receipts from nonfederal sources. Appropriations fell short of the authorization in the first year, fiscal 1971, and provided the $20 million plus $3 million mentioned earlier. For the following year, with an authorization already on the books, the administration called for full funding and the Congress granted the funds. In addition, the president's budget message promised that the long-deferred plan for regular, long-term funding for public broadcasting would be forwarded to Congress in the course of the 1971 calendar year. When the appropriations were enacted with record speed and funds were actually available in advance of June 30, the coming year held high promise. CPB's available funding would be $40 million (a more than seven-fold increase in four years), and the long-range proposal could be expected as an even more favorable sign for the future.

In my early conversations with Dean Burch, the FCC chairman appointed in 1969, his interest in public broadcasting was apparent, and he encouraged a continuing dialogue with CPB about future financing. He was particularly intrigued by the concept of more direct viewer contributions to financing as utilized by the British and Japanese. Ever since the early days of radio in the United Kingdom, the BBC had been financed through an annual license charge for each receiver. This sum was increased from time to time—particularly after the advent of television—and collected by the postmaster general. The Japanese adopted the practice of bimonthly subscription charges, similar to utility payments, which were billed and collected by the public broadcasting system, NHK. This user charge approach had the appeal of these successful models and the logic of direct payment by the user of the service to be financed. The consulting firm of Arthur D. Little, which had performed the cost analysis for the Carnegie Commission four years earlier, was engaged by CPB to study the feasibility of this approach. Although the study was helpful as an updating of the financial problem, its findings were most discouraging. The cost of collection and enforcement of the user charge, however it was labeled, was deemed excessive. Negative consumer reaction in a culture where television was considered a free service would heighten prospects of evasion. More research was added; no solution was found.

In a display of understandable impatience, Congressman

Robert Tiernan, a member of the House subcommittee, requested the FCC, HEW, and CPB to study ways for providing long-range financing and to submit recommendations to Congress. CPB responded, in September 1970, with recommendations similar to those delivered the previous year to the administration: the dedicated excise tax and the matching formula as deposit for a public broadcasting fund. No recommendations came from the government sources. Tiernan introduced a bill with the CPB provisions in 1970. When no action occurred, he reintroduced it the following year, but without the excise tax. Congressional initiative had at least been demonstrated.

OFFICE OF TELECOMMUNICATIONS POLICY

This initiative was paralleled in time by the formation of a new executive agency, the Office of Telecommunications Policy (OTP). The new agency was created by the reorganization plan route and was destined to play a key role in the formulation and presentation of administration policy in this area. OTP was soon headed by Clay T. Whitehead, a systems analyst and management science practitioner, who had been the White House staffer on communications under Robert Ellsworth and later under Peter Flanigan. The agency, as described in the president's message accompanying the plan, was intended to develop policy to "take advantage of the nation's technological capabilities," to assure the best utilization of government frequencies, and "to enable the executive branch to speak with a clearer voice and to act as a more effective partner with both the Congress and the FCC." This last grant of discretion was broad enough to permit OTP to assume the executive branch leadership in determining the administration position on public broadcasting and its federal funding.

Consultation on a future plan centered in OTP starting late in 1970. Previous positions in FCC, HEW, and the Budget Bureau were tied together under Whitehead's leadership. From the start of these discussions it was evident that the new office was not concerned exclusively with the funding route for public broadcasting, but more fundamentally with a *de novo* assessment of the public policy issues that formed the foundation for the 1967 act and the creation of CPB and its public mission. Should the federal government be involved at all in broadcasting? If so, in what areas, under what organizational structure within and outside government? To what extent should a national organization—CPB—decide system policy independent of government accountability? What alternate means to federal funding could be identified? Why was the system unable to function within the classic concept of the marketplace? If citizens want public television, why shouldn't they voluntarily pay what it costs to deliver it? By the same reasoning, if stations desired national programs, why shouldn't they pay the cost rather than have a national organization decide for them, buy the programs, and send those programs through the interconnection?

Although these were perfectly appropriate, basic questions to raise, they were difficult for public broadcasting advocates to accept. Public broadcasting advocates believed that the answers had been set forth in the 1967 act, and that administration support since that time constituted acceptance of those answers. The discussions were not entirely satisfactory to either party. The draft bill that emerged from OTP, after six months of discussion, was not long-range financing. Instead, it was a sweeping amendment to the act, with the intention of reducing the scope of CPB functions and discretion. CPB would be barred from educational projects in favor of the Office of Education— which was to be more actively engaged in broadcasting— and from action in new technology beyond over-the-air broadcasting. The funds available to CPB would be expended under limitations; the station grants would be automatically distributed in accordance with formulas prescribed in the statute. The CPB response was negative, as were comments from HEW and the FCC, and the CPB board requested renewed consideration of plans to finance the system under existing conditions. Early decision was urged, to permit enactment of extended authorization before the end of the 1971 congressional session. Without authorization, the entire funding process in 1972 would be delayed, with the consequent lag in future planning.

THE GUILTY VERDICT AT MIAMI BEACH

No plan was forthcoming. No new position was offered by the administration. Repeated efforts by CPB board members over a ninety day period to discuss the issue with Whitehead were frustrated. The verdict, however, was handed down—without advance warning or consultation —in a Whitehead speech to the assembled station managers at the NAEB convention in Miami Beach in late October of 1971. It was an indictment of the system developed under CPB leadership in the previous three years. It accused CPB and PBS of excessive centralization through the formation of the "fourth network" and the arbitrary selection and distribution of scheduled national programs. Condemning the CPB priority support of interconnection and national programming, Whitehead called for a return to "the bed-rock of localism" in much larger and statutory-based grants to stations. He attacked Ford Foundation support of public affairs programs and questioned the "objectivity and balance" of video journalism. He offered no guidance with respect to future funding but warned that further developments along existing lines would assure that "permanent financing will always be somewhere off in the distant future."

The atmosphere, both inside and outside the system, changed. Inside it was divisive. Whitehead had encouraged the stations to seek a higher priority and larger share of CPB funds and to police programs from the national level. The nature of the relationship between CPB and PBS had been attacked, and the justification for interconnection had been questioned. The intrusion of political forces, long feared as a probable companion to federal involvement, had become a reality. In reaction to the speech and to the administration's abandonment of the long-range financing proposal promised by the president in 1971, Congressman Macdonald introduced his own authorization bill, which would provide five years funding at rising levels from $65 million in 1973 to $145.5 million in 1978. The political lines were drawn. The system's pattern of development had been openly challenged by the administration, and a Democratic congressional spokesman and system advocate had responded.

In his speech, Whitehead invited station managers to come directly to him to discuss the system's future. They did. Initially heartened by his apparent understanding of their financial plight and his sympathetic support for their mounting pressure to gain a larger slice of the CPB pie, they were discouraged over their inability to secure any administration commitment on future financing. When the president's budget displayed $45 million as the level for fiscal year 1973 and the administration authorization bill requested only a one-year extension, they were disappointed. Even the $10 million increase had emerged after extensive behind-the-scenes negotiation between CPB board members and White House representatives. Some advance understandings concerning use of that increase—primarily increased station grants and no national program expansion—were necessary to assure its insertion in the budget. Even so, when the board reaffirmed its commitment to public affairs programs in January 1972, the authorization bill was revised on the eve of its transmittal to Congress. The revision included the punitive amendment prescribing a statutory pattern to govern the allocation of funds for station grants, thereby reducing the corporation's discretion in determining systemwide needs. The interplay of funding and program decisions had been "made absolutely clear."

EVERYBODY UNDERSTANDS SALARY FIGURES

Another financial crisis added flavor to these days of dispute. The revelation of Vanocur's salary set off a chain reaction of congressional requests for salary information about other performers and executives in public broadcasting. The collection of such information by CPB from independent elements in the system met with resistance and delay that heightened the demand. When the information was released, it revealed that a handful of on-air performers and executives were receiving salaries above the congressional level of $42,500. Even such backers of public broadcasting as Senator Pastore deplored these salaries as out of line with government. The ability of the corporation to operate as an independent, nongovernment agency was in doubt. Government funds generated a tide that carried it toward the federal shore and away from the private shore. The CPB board reacted with a resolution requiring its review and approval of all salaries in excess of $36,000 that were to be paid from its funds. In an assertion of its right to function independently as a nongovernmental entity, CPB reiterated its intention to compensate the corporation's president at $65,000 regardless of critical comment in some quarters. Subsequently, on the House floor a limitation on CPB salaries was passed as an amendment to the authorization bill.

A blow by blow account of the 1972 legislative rounds would consume more time than patience could justify. Those with intense interest in the problems inherent in the treatment of the system's issues in the congressional arena will find a study of the hearing record and committee reports and particularly the extensive floor debates to be revealing.

From this process of public exposure and debate several conclusions must be drawn.

(1) Even more system-wide collaboration was necessary to gain common advocacy before governmental authorities. The failure of the corporation to assure station acceptance of the broad financial plan represented in the Macdonald bill and of the station representatives to formulate their own common advocacy emphasized the cleavage within the system and weakened its effectiveness in dealing with basic policy questions. The multiplicity and fragmentation of organizations rendered the type of responsive action necessary in a fast moving legislative situation virtually impossible.

At the initial hearings before the Macdonald subcommittee, station representatives challenged the portion of the proposed authorization committed to station grants. They contended that more than the 30 percent already assured was a more accurate reflection of total system need. However, they were not able to agree among themselves as to whether the amount required was 40 percent, 50 percent, or even 75 percent. And when queried as to the public purposes to be served by such a level of funding, their brief was unimpressive.

The tensions in the system, heightened by the White-head rhetoric, revealed an absence of confidence on the part of the stations with respect to CPB decisions on fund distribution for the system. As the legislation was shaped, new demands were made for more direct participation by station managers in these decisions. The inclusion of concurrence by station representatives with respect to CPB fund distribution as a statutory requirement was advocated by NAEB leaders.

Out of these complications during the House hearings came a CPB board-approved plan, in March 1972, for much greater and more direct station participation in system financial and policy planning. The plan assured stations that at least 30 percent of CPB funds at the $40 million level would be distributed in community service grants, with the understanding that higher percentages might be expected as the total climbed to the higher amounts set forth in the Macdonald bill. The formula for distribution of these grants would be jointly determined by station managers and CPB management, with opportunity for the managers to appeal to the CPB board if agreement could not be reached. In addition, a special committee of twelve station representatives would henceforth participate in the entire budget formulation process starting with fiscal year 1974. This would permit station input in the development of planning assumptions and criteria, the pricing of the assumptions, the determination of options, and the final selection of priorities. Reservations or objections to final decisions could be argued before the board prior to the submission of the final budget requests to the government.

This expansion of participative democracy in the governance of the system was accepted by the station representatives, and the new processes were adopted for immediate application. The pattern of shared decision making produced a new unity within the system in support of the modified bill, which was ultimately passed by both houses of Congress.

But this degree of station involvement at the national level was still not sufficient to meet congressional views of the system's leadership. This was evident in the amendment to the bill which required that five of the fifteen CPB board members nominated by the president would in the future be "station members." While not openly opposing this amendment, CPB objected to it. The corporation preferred the involvement of station representation on the collaborative basis already accepted internally, without the shared accountability which was inherent in the required board membership for the corporation. In the board's carefully cast words, prepared for use at congressional hearings, it was its "view that it will find the means to seek and obtain the advice of the stations on all matters of interest to them, and that this approach is preferable to the mandatory appointment of station managers or any other specific group of individuals to the corporation's board or to limiting the independence of the board by requiring any outside group to express its concurrence or consent to actions taken by the board."

The concern of the stations about the legislation brought renewed attempts at collective action by station board chairmen. Earlier moves in this direction had aborted because of the part-time service of board members, the apprehension of managers over combined power of board chairmen, and the diversity of licensee governance. But the necessity to represent constituent viewers before congressional committees called for testimony from those responsible for the local license. The board chairman, rather than the manager, could exercise that responsibility as a spokesman for the audience. As the Macdonald bill moved along, so did the formation of "a loosely knit organization" of board chairmen under the guidance of the chairman for the Dallas station, Ralph Rogers. An expanded assemblage of this organization—representing more than fifty stations —had just concluded its mobilization meeting in Scottsdale, Arizona, when the veto was delivered. At that meeting, the chairmen had committed themselves to encourage board members to become more active in building a broad support for public broadcasting. These responsible directors concluded that they could more accurately and forcefully represent the citizen interest in public television than could the station managers, whose professional future was so inexorably related to improved federal support.

(2) That FOB factor was to be applied. Opponents of public affairs programs, although not a majority in Congress, were a vocal minority—particularly when urged on by the administration. In the hearings and on the floor Congressman Springer and Senator Baker, ranking Republicans in this policy area, forcefully reiterated the

necessity for "strict adherence" to the factor and seriously questioned whether it had been observed as literally as Congress had intended. Some members were determined to take legal action against those who produced or transmitted programs judged to violate FOB. The House amendment prohibiting use of public opinion polls reflected this apprehension and also the willingness of Congress to introduce restrictions on the free play of video journalism.

Doubt was left, however, concerning the precise definition of these standards. Those who were obliged to interpret the standards realized that eventually regulatory or judicial review would be required to give meaning to such general terms and their relation to existing fairness doctrine standards. The insistence on application of the factor, combined with confusion over its definition, would chill the initiative of the journalist and deepen the caution in public affairs programming. These conditions appeared to respond to the administration's wishes and the minority concerns in Congress.

(3) The failure of CPB to finance program projects more directly associated with classroom instruction or with educational objectives tended to retard the growth of congressional support.

(4) Although long-range financing remained the rallying objective and the restrictions of annual appropriations were recognized, there was no unanimity with respect to devices for such financing or with respect to the federal government as the principal source of that funding. Even congressional advocates of the system interpreted long-range as meaning nonfederal. This marginal tendency toward withdrawal from federal reliance and involvement may have been a temporary attitude, but it was probably

motivated by distaste or criticism in relation to some programming or, more philosophically, by rising apprehension over potential federal intrusion in program judgments no matter how the federal dollars entered the system.

In spite of these reservations and signals of doubt, and after all of the hours of debate, there was general approval of system progress to date and a desire to enlarge and protect it. The volume of objections was not the voice of consensus. Apathy, misunderstanding, and confusion were more serious factors in the passage of legislation than hostility and disagreement. The depth of citizen interest in public television financed by the federal government had still not been demonstrated sufficiently to members of Congress to sustain their commitment. The good word from the home district had not been received with sufficient frequency and intensity to justify extra interest in this item in competition with other issues on their crowded agenda.

The Macdonald bill was finally passed in the Senate on June 22 and sent to the president. It emerged as an authorization for two more years at funding levels of $65 million in 1973 and $90 million in 1974. It carried the amendment to provide station members on the board along with the salary and polling limitations. The action had been speeded by the Senate rejecting its own amendments and accepting the House version to avoid a conference for resolution of differences between the bills. The House had finally passed the bill 256 to 69 after a few close votes on amendments. The administration amendment to reduce the authorization to a single year and the amount to $40 million had been defeated by the slim margin of 183 to 166.

The final Senate passage was by a 82 to 1 vote; the only dissenter was Senator James Buckley, whose brother's program was to be financed under a spending plan predicated on the authorization.

THE VETO

Eight days later the bill was vetoed by President Nixon, just as Congress recessed for the Democratic convention. While stating that "public broadcasting deserved to be continued and to be strengthened," the president judged the legislation to be "a poor approach to public broadcast financing" because it ignored some serious questions which must be resolved before any long-range public broadcasting financing can be soundly devised and before the statutory framework for public broadcasting is changed. The national versus local dispute was cited. The text of the President's veto message expressed it in these terms:

There are many fundamental disagreements concerning the directions which public broadcasting has taken and should pursue in the future. Perhaps the most important one is the serious and widespread concern—expressed in Congress and within public broadcasting itself—that an organization, originally intended only to serve the local stations, is becoming the center of power and focal point of control for the entire public broadcasting system.

The Public Broadcasting Act of 1967 made localism a primary means of achieving the goals of the educational broadcasting system. Localism places the principal public interest responsibility on the individual educational radio and television stations licensed to serve the needs and interest of their own communities. By not placing adequate emphasis on localism, the bill threatens to erode substantially public broadcasting's impressive potential for promoting innovative and diverse cultural and educational programming.

This was a delayed rerun of the Whitehead verdict at Miami Beach eight months earlier. It showed little understanding of the actual system structure and operations with the station as the essential element.

The disapproval was also based on need for more time and experience with the system prior to more extensive funding. In defense of his administration's record, President Nixon cited the growth from $5 million in fiscal year 1969 to $35 million in 1972 and restated his request for $45 million, a 30 percent increase for the coming year. Pointing out that the vetoed bill would "almost double next year's appropriation, and more than doubles the following year's appropriation over 1972," he described the funding in the bill as unwarranted in light of the serious questions yet unanswered by our brief experience with public broadcasting."

But there was no specification in the message of what answers or objectives were deemed proper by the administration. The prospect of early initiative on long-range financing—despite administration assurance in hearing testimony that a plan would be submitted prior to the end of the one year authorization, June 30, 1973—was indeed bleak when the message concluded with: "I urge the continuation of carefully measured annual funding for the corporation, under the existing statutory framework, subject to regular budgetary oversight and review."

The veto was a watershed; a point of transition. Although Congressman Macdonald exploded with righteous wrath and NAEB expressed its dissent, there was no inclination or spirit to charge forth and attempt to override the veto.

The CPB board was so worried about alternate funding that they made no move to challenge the president's indictment of their stewardship and were willing to accept this retardation in the system's growth. While the legislative mill was grinding on the authorization bill, three new appointees and two reappointees to the board were nominated by the President and confirmed by the Senate. The Network Project, a group of activist students at Columbia University, raised the only question about the nominees when their representative repeated the substance of their earlier charge in the still pending suit against the corporation.[1] It was their brief at the confirmation hearing that these nominees, as well as the other board members, did not sufficiently represent the public and did not possess enough of the qualifications set forth in the statute. A similar pattern of appointments and reappointments had been followed by the president in 1970 to give the board a decided Nixon complexion: seven appointees (Albert Cole had been named by Nixon to succeed Milton Eisenhower in 1969); four reappointees; four original Johnson appointees (Pace, Killian, Valenti, and Benjamin).

CPB REACTION TO VETO

At its first meeting, three weeks after the veto, the CPB board resolved

that it urge early action by Congress to assure adequate financing for public broadcasting in fiscal year 1973. Due to the needs of public broadcasting, with particular emphasis on the needs of local radio and television stations for increased community service grants, the board feels that a $55 million au-

[1] The Network Project had brought suit in federal district court in New York against CPB and PBS in December of 1971. It charged that the Public Broadcasting Act and the first amendment had been violated by CPB/PBS national program selection and distribution. These particular charges were withdrawn by the plaintiff in June of 1973 after legal jousting out of court, and new, more sweeping charges were filed in the district court in the District of Columbia.

thorization and appropriation is essential to maintain present levels of activity. The board also reemphasized its determination to seek, in conjunction with all elements of the industry, Congress, and the administration, adequate long-range financing to assure continued growth and development of public broadcasting as it matures toward its rightful position as a positive force for service to the American people.

This split-the-difference effort was nonproductive. The administration bill was passed, but without the punitive section added earlier. The appropriation process stalled, however, when the HEW–Labor bill in which the CPB money was buried became a central battleground between the president and Congress. The result was two more vetoes. Rarely in the annals of government has one institution been victimized by presidential veto thrice in a single session. To this day, more than eight months into the present fiscal year, there is no appropriation. The delay has caused the administration to lower the final request to the continuing resolution level—the same as fiscal year 1972—of $35 million. The prospect for 1974 is little brighter. The president's budget requests $45 million once again; there is no sign of an authorization request and certainly no trace of a beginning on long-range funding.[2]

AFTER CPB LEADERSHIP CHANGES

The veto generated leadership change. I resigned as president in August, convinced that my incompatibility with administration positions would endanger the system and that I was not prepared to play that patsy role in which *Variety* had cast me. A new board chairman was selected at the September annual meeting, when Frank

[2] Subsequently an authorization request was forthcoming, from the administration, for another one-year extension at $45 million. Two year extensions, with dollar figures roughly the same as those vetoed in 1973, were introduced in the House and the Senate.

Pace withdrew his candidacy for reelection by his colleagues after four and one-half years of service. The board elected as chairman its newest member, Thomas Curtis, an eighteen-year Republican congressman who, since his defeat at the hands of Thomas Eagleton in the 1968 race for the Senate, had been practicing law and serving as an executive with the Encyclopedia Britannica. At the same meeting the board designated a new president, Henry Loomis, the deputy director of the United States Information Agency (USIA) and former director of the Voice of America, to succeed me.

When the prospects for genuine long-range financing dimmed in early 1972, and after CPB witnesses had been berated for their failure to initiate such plans in recognition of administration unwillingness to take that essential step, the CPB board concluded that an industry-wide study and position development was overdue. If that second phase in the original intent of 1967 was ever to be achieved, the public broadcasting enterprise would have to prepare a common plan which all elements of the system could endorse and to negotiate with executive and congressional leaders on the basis of such terms. With the backing of all system organizations, a task force was formed of fourteen representatives of all elements under the chairmanship of Joseph Hughes, a recently reappointed board member. The new leadership of the corporation encouraged the work of the task force and articulated their commitment to press for action.

FINDING ASSUMPTIONS FOR AN IDEAL SYSTEM

To guide their study and debate, the task force set the assumptions for an ideal system that could be adequately and appropriately funded. First, they projected 90 percent coverage of national population, recognizing that the cost of reaching that last 10 percent was prohibitive and recommending that other technology—cable and satellite —be considered for that remote sector.

Second, federal support should be limited to 35 to 50 percent of the system operating needs. This was an arbitrary and pragmatic judgment but formed in the belief that this range would not constitute undue influence or control.

Third, on the capital side—because there is less sensitivity in dealing with hardware—the federal share could be advanced to 50 to 75 percent.

From these assumptions, projections were calculated:

(1) To achieve 90 percent coverage would require a total capital investment for television of *$534 million*. With 1972 accumulated capital expenditures at $230 million, an additional *$304 million* would be required to complete the ideal system, and *$70 million* would be needed to cover depreciation and replacement.

(2) Using 50 percent as a federal share, the requirement was roughly *$152 million* for capital expenses and *$35 million* for depreciation from the federal treasury.

(3) Total operating costs are estimated at *$475 million* annually. Employing the assumed ratio of 30 to 50 percent, annual federal support would range from *$166 to $237.5 million*.

These calculations are remarkably close to the Carnegie Commission projections adjusted for the five-year inflation rate.

BASIC PRINCIPLES TO SUPPORT LONG-RANGE FINANCING

In their struggle to design a funding plan, the task force enunciated a list of basic principles as a system framework.

Many principles were reaffirmations of past criteria, but they had the higher value of agreement and support from all parties in the system and of current evaluation:

(1) The principal share of the operating expenses of public broadcasting should continue to come from non-federal sources. But it is entirely appropriate and necessary that federal funds be a part of a total financing plan.

(2) The federal contribution should be designed so that it provides incentives for increasing nonfederal financing.

(3) Financing of public broadcasting should not impose unreasonable burdens upon any segment of the economy, but rather should be designed so that those who benefit also pay.

(4) If federal funds are appropriated in whole or in part by a matching system, a portion of those funds should be returned to the stations on an equitable basis which reflects local effort.

(5) If federal funds are appropriated, there will need to be accountability to the Congress in the use of these funds.

(6) The need for insulation against undue pressures from whatever source is particularly important with respect to the financing of programming.

(7) Long-range planning, which is based on a reasonably assured level of future funding, is essential to a viable public broadcasting industry capable of producing high quality services and programs, locally and nationally.

(8) The financing of facilities is as urgent as the financing of operating expenses, and the funding level must be increased to meet system needs.

(9) It is both appropriate and vital that private under-

writing of local and national program costs continues as an important method of financing.

(10) The development of a plan for the system's growth, the strengthening of local planning and management capabilities, and the setting of priorities which can be translated into specific local and national objectives are all essential to the achievement of long-range financing.

(11) The development of a strong and effective public broadcasting industry requires that the Corporation for Public Broadcasting continue to play a leadership role as envisioned in the Public Broadcasting Act of 1967.

(12) Any long-range financing plan should be flexible enough to permit participation in cable, satellites, and other new technologies.

ROLL CALL OF FINANCIAL MODES

The full list of past financing modes was evaluated individually and in combination:

(1) a dedicated excise tax on the sale of receivers;

(2) a tax on commercial station gross revenues or advertising revenues;

(3) a charge on commercial broadcasters for access to the broadcast spectrum;

(4) a setting aside of a portion of the income taxes paid by commercial operators;

(5) a dedicated excise tax on residential electric or telephone bills;

(6) a share of the proceeds from the profits of operating a domestic satellite system;

(7) a user charge to be paid by families owning sets;

(8) general tax revenues based on a statutory formula and legislated on either a permanent or multi-year authorization and appropriations basis;

(9) a direct matching plan, such as one by which the federal government would provide a specified match for every dollar raised by the system from nonfederal sources; and

(10) the sale of federally guaranteed bonds that would produce supplementary revenue.

TO PREFER THE MATCHING MODE

Because of despair over dedicated taxation prospects, primary task force attention is being directed toward matching, bond sales, and general tax revenues on a multiyear basis. Matching is again the favorite. Endless variations are possible. The group of station board chairmen has suggested a simple plan of fifty federal cents for each nonfederal dollar in the system—a flashback to the almost identical CPB proposal of 1969. Simplicity and incentive value are cited to advance the matching proposal. But there is also the pragmatic understanding that plans of this type have gained favor with Congress and, although such plans are counter to administration opposition to category grants, they have not been rejected by the executive.

It is open season on public broadcasting financing plans. Hartford Gunn, PBS president, devoted his experience to the development of an alternate plan. His plan would place most of the federal funds for programs in the hands of the stations for their investment through a cooperative, presumably PBS, in desired national programming. The CPB role would be reduced to more limited system-wide functions and removed from any involvement in financing of program selection. This plan deserves close study, because an adaptation of it may be incorporated in or combined with other financing plans. Clearly, an increased injection of market economics would strengthen responsiveness of producers and distributors to the consuming station needs while complicating the resolution of conflicting taste and possibly curbing the generation of new and innovative program ideas. This economic concept can only be accepted if it will stimulate the development of program content truly in accord with citizen needs and will promote high quality and broad diversity. If federal funds are involved, creative freedom must be assured while accountability is rendered to the taxpayer.

That is the financial picture behind the picture on the public tube. Progress, disappointment, expectations, frustrations, rising resources and rising costs, agreement and division—all are dabs of color in this picture. Those who advocate and those who oppose the medium need to study not only the numbers but how the numbers were shaped and what they are intended to produce. The vast mixture of dollar users and dollar sources affords new vistas of diversity and pluralism. Can these generally accepted virtues become the touchstone of this potent carrier of public service? The answer must be *yes* if this system is to survive and serve. In the final chapter I pursue and hopefully set forth the imperatives for progress in public television; I seek to array those imperatives on a course that will secure the public communications dividend.

IV

To Secure the Public's Communication Dividend: Imperatives for Progress in Public Television

System structure, programming, and financing for public television have undergone change in the five years since Congress passed the Public Broadcasting Act. Today, with the elements in the structure under close reexamination, the program substance under critical reevaluation, and the financing patterns under task force exploration, the system is moving toward a new stage. Whether that stage is growth toward a more viable system of public service, continuing internal uncertainty and conflict, or a return to fragmented localism must be determined soon, or progress achieved to date will be sacrificed and this instrument for public benefit will slip away. It may become a noble idea that could not find a meaningful fulfillment in our contemporary society.

In discussing improvements in any system, those seeking the improvements all too frequently fail to consider those who should be the beneficiaries of that system. Students are sometimes overlooked when educational changes are considered. Patients are not necessarily the central concern in designs for improved health care. Passenger comfort and convenience are frequently forgotten in the development of transportation systems. It is unhappily the cultural tendency of public service institutions to assume a life of their own, without adequate reference to those for whom they were established to serve. Decisions tend to be formed more to serve those within the institution or to strengthen some feature of the institution without relation to its service goals. These institutional tendencies have been manifest in exaggerated form in recent television history. Internal political positioning, intramural contests, facilities acquisition, program choices, financial accumulation and distribution, and other prevalent activities which have dominated the scene behind the camera may have only limited impact on the purpose of the entire venture—benefits to the citizen viewer at home, school, work site, or wherever that ubiquitous receiver is located. The public itself, the "public" in public broadcasting, has been forgotten more often than remembered.

Dominance by the public is an imperative in this system's development, not just as a slogan but as a conscious planning and operating objective. That public should be viewed as individuals and groups with interests, desires, and needs that can be effectively approached through the delivery of program services in sight and sound by electronic means. It should not be viewed as a prospective consumer of goods who can be motivated to buy through the merchandising process of home entertainment.

This is the public—a mosaic formed of the human diversity of our society. It is not a composite man or woman, the middle American, some statistical mean, an intelligence norm toward which programs are beamed. It is the individuals, the families, the social groups that make up the audience before that screen. The purpose of the enterprise must be to reach that audience with opportunities for education and enlightenment, information and different entertainment. These opportunities must be available to everyone—young and old; majority and minority; affluent, middle income, and poor; local, regional, and national; man, woman, and child—all 200 million citizens.

CAPACITY TO REACH THE PUBLIC

With this purpose in mind, what is the existing physical capability of the system to reach the public with this opportunity? The rapid growth of stations by local initiative and without national plan has extended the reach. It is possible for any local group to file with the FCC for one of the channels reserved for educational use. The license will be issued with minimum evidence of educational purpose and financial capability. If the sponsoring group can raise 25 percent of the capital facilities cost, it can qualify to stand in line at HEW for the balance in federal funds. Once a group has the plant and enters the broadcast spectrum, it is eligible for a CPB community service grant to augment locally generated operating support. The number of stations increased from 56 in 1961 to 117 in 1966, 207 in 1971, and 227 in 1972.

What does this station population represent in public coverage? The addition of new stations would seem to mean more viewers reached, but this is not always true. The absence of national planning means that there have been overlapping licensees, for example in New York, the San Francisco Bay area, North Carolina, the Salt Lake City area, and even metropolitan Tampa, while large sections are totally uncovered. But as of November 1, 1971, with 212 (90 VHF, 122 UHF) stations on the air, public broadcasting was providing a signal which included within its coverage contour about 71.5 percent of the total population or about *148 million* Americans. Additional coverage since that date should raise the total to *156 million*, or approximately 75 percent of the population. The band location numbers are significant, because coverage potential must be reduced if the assigned channel is in the UHF band. In a 1971 study for CPB, the Louis Harris organization discounted for the UHF penetration problem and cut back total coverage to 63 percent or *131.5 million* potential viewers.

Theoretically, the system should offer opportunity to every single citizen. The cost of such absolute coverage would be prohibitive by over-the-air transmission; preliminary estimates call for almost a doubling of capital costs to reach the widely scattered, low concentration areas which constitute the last 10 percent. If 90 percent coverage is accepted as a reasonable goal—and I believe it should be accepted and defended—it will cover all population in geographic areas in excess of one hundred thousand with broadcast television of a national, regional, and local character through 339 stations or transmitters. To achieve this level of opportunity, 112 additional transmitters with nonduplicating coverage would have to be licensed and activated. This compares with the Carnegie Commission's 1966 estimate of 380 stations by 1976. It would be realistic, in view of capital requirements, to assume that another five to eight years would be required to complete this coverage. In the meantime, other means of transmission could be developed to provide the equivalent service through other technological processes. In any event, the cable process should be actively explored to serve in smaller communities where public broadcasting cannot be financially viable.

NEED FOR STATION BIRTH CONTROL

This station increase necessitates more planned parenthood than has been practiced in recent times. Unless there is agreement on "birth control," expensive capital equipment and services will be acquired for new stations that overlap existing service or that are in communities unable to support them without disproportionate national assistance. In the past two years, CPB and PBS have been faced with demands for service to the new stations. Those demands diluted their resources without significant benefit to the public. Restraint on local initiative is difficult to justify when there are so many communication needs to be met. But it is not a free market in the traditional sense, and public interest limits are necessary and desirable.

The trend toward more statewide service is encouraging as a means for increasing coverage with minimum expenditures for capital and operations. Transmitters can be located—as they are in states like South Carolina, Nebraska, and Kentucky—to achieve total coverage with program origination at a single central point. This pattern has been adopted or is being planned in Maryland, New Jersey, Louisiana, and other states. Economies of scale can be achieved in this manner without totally usurping local options for service. Likewise, regional combinations in areas like the Rocky Mountains may prove effective in reaching uncovered communities through assistance and cooperative programming.

Station representatives, through NAEB and PBS, should meet with the FCC, HEW, and OTP, to develop an acceptable plan for future station growtr during the next ten years, with due regard for possible technological advances during that period. In the interest of system-wide participation in these planning decisions, the present task force on long-range financing—which has already adopted the 90 percent target—could be the organizational means by which this plan could be developed and subsequently monitored and modified to match changing conditions.

	1960	*1962*	*1964*	*1966*	*1968*	*1970*	*1971*
Station reporting	56	62	88	115	153	190	193
Average broadcast hours per station per week	39.0	41.9	42.3	49.5	56.1	65.3	74.6

SOURCE: Financial Statistics of Public Television Licensee, Fiscal Year 1971, National Center for Educational Statistics and Corporation for Public Broadcasting.

More important, in quantitative terms, than the number and coverage of transmitters is the volume of programming carried by the broadcast signals. For the sake of time-to-time contrast, it is interesting to note that in 1961, when 56 stations were on the air, a little more than 2,100 hours of programs were transmitted in an average week, whereas in 1971, the 207 stations were broadcasting over 12,650 hours per week, an increase of more than sixfold. In fiscal year 1971, the total hours per station per week ranged from 74.6 in school weeks to 44.2 in the summer season:

	Peak season (35–36 weeks) (hours per week)	*Summer season (16–17 weeks) (hours per week)*
Community	79.2	47.4
School system	62.1	40.2
State	81.7	45.8
University	68.0	42.0

SOURCE: Financial Statistics of Public Television Licensees, Fiscal Year 1971, National Center for Educational Statistics and Corporation for Public Broadcasting.

School programming is still an essential component of service and is reflected in the seasonal differences. For the full year, school service totaled 226,165 hours, or 35.4 percent, and general programming intended for nonclassroom use totaled 413,446 hours, or 64.4 percent. Even the community stations, which as a group have the most limited classroom commitment, transmitted 58,864 hours, or 32.4 percent of their time to schools. In future planning, it should be assumed that school demands will be for one-third of the broadcast hours. That figure may be reduced, not through fewer school hours but more general broadcast hours. Many stations have not been able to afford the cost of program operations for weekend service and have presented blank faces during some of the most popular viewing hours. The first national program distributions were built around Sunday evening, to give the stations the substance for that prime time. Later PBS distributed children's programs on Saturday morning to fill that time with "Sesame Street," "Electric Company," and "Misteroger's Neighborhood." By these supportive moves, more program hours of high quality can be added to the station's service schedule. It should be the goal of each station to have a signal of service for up to 18 hours per day, 7 days per week, or a total of 126 hours per week. That total objective would increase viewer opportunities by more than 50 hours from the 1971 weekly average of 74.6 hours in peak season. These are the expanded target areas for local, regional, and national programming in response to public need.

IS ANYBODY WATCHING?

These are the opportunities offered the public. To what extent is the public already seizing them? Is anyone really watching public television? Richard Doan, the perceptive commentator in "TV Guide," asked this question in 1971, and then, applying commercial broadcasting audience measures, answered "not very many." Is public broadcasting attracting any group other than the so-called elite with high earnings and higher education? I recall that at the time of my entry into public broadcasting one critic told me that I was not engaging in a public service because "after all, public broadcasting is the poverty program for the overly educated."

Interest in audience numbers can be misunderstood. One of the Whitehead points of attack was that public broadcasting was competing with the commercial broadcasters for audience because from time to time its leaders conducted and publicized audience research.

Most of the existing television audience research has been designed for commercial use. It is heavily oriented toward mass market measurement, with recent interest in "demographics" to pinpoint audience elements as advertising targets. The almost blind faith placed in these survey results is scarcely justified by the process and techniques used, and certainly such surveys are not the final answer in public broadcasting. They have been used to provide crude measures and to form the bases for time-to-time comparisons on reasonably fixed terms.

In 1971, Harris audience studies commissioned by CPB did reveal that public television was being watched—and by an increasing number of Americans and for longer periods of time each day. Using a national sample of more than 2,000 people, the Louis Harris organization estimated that 39 million persons watched public television at least once a week in 1971. Because this was the third consecutive year of this survey, it could be used to plot a trend—

from 24 million in 1969, to 33 million in 1970 to the 39 million in 1971, or an increase of 62 percent in two years and of 19 percent in the past year.

Harris found that median hours of viewing, although only at 1.9 hours a week, had increased from 1.4 hours the previous year. The survey showed a dramatic increase in viewing by Blacks. In 1970, 35 percent of Black householders said they watched their local public television station. By 1971, that figure rose to 52 percent. The highest concentration of viewers are between the ages of 21 and 29 and live chiefly in the cities and suburbs. Sixty-one percent of college graduates interviewed said they watched, and 28 percent of those who never completed high school also declared themselves viewers. By income, 55 percent of those earning $15,000 or more watch public television, and so do 29 percent of those whose incomes are less than $5,000 per year. Thus, although there is clearly greater interest in PTV among better-educated and high-income earners, the other end of the education and income range is by no means outside of the audience.

Views about PTV highlighted by the survey offer some insights concerning the citizen viewer and his attitude:

30 percent of the respondents said they thought they were wasting too much time watching commercial television, but only 17 percent of public television viewers felt that way;

43 percent felt that commercial stations often present biased points of view, but only 16 percent felt that way about PTV; and

35 percent of the total sample thought their local public television station presents all points of view, but only 7 percent believed it tends to present a particular point of view.

This and other studies, both national and local (the most significant local survey was conducted by KQED, in conjunction with Stanford, in the San Francisco Bay area with a telephone sample of over 30,000) indicate that, although public television's audience is small by the mass audience standards of commercial broadcasters, the PTV audience is nonetheless significant and increasing. The number watching any one program may be relatively low, but the cumulative viewing over a week's time is high. This tends to support the contention that viewing is selective and that programming should be designed to appeal to target groups composed of minority slices of the population. As one station programmer expressed it, "I would never expect our viewers to stay with our schedule for an entire evening; I would never do that myself."

One method of audience response, a measure of intensity of interest, is the announcement that a particular program may not be funded and must leave the air. When a fund cutback threatened "World Press" continuation in 1971 and that dismal prospect was forecast on the program, several thousand communications of protest—and even a few dollar contributions—were received. An unusually large number came from teachers, who explained that they used the program as home viewing in social studies or current events classes and would be seriously deprived by the loss of it.

A more recent test came in January 1973, when CPB announced it might not be able to continue support for NPACT's production of "Washington Week in Review," apparently because of White House objection to regular correspondent Peter Lisagor's tough assessment of presidential performance. This uncertainty about the program's continuation was mentioned on-air, and within two weeks NPACT received over fifteen thousand pleas for continued service. So the occasional comment that no one is watching or that no one cares can be specifically refuted.

More scientific audience research is needed at all levels. More information is needed about viewer reaction beyond the identification of those who watch. The NIMH study of violence on TV—made by HEW after pressure from Senator Pastore—and the Eisenhower Commission that studied violence after the assassinations in 1968 demonstrated how difficult and potentially disappointing such research can be. Both studies concluded that violence on television had adverse impact on the behavior of children who witnessed acts of video violence, and that it contributed to the acceptance of antisocial reactions toward others. But researchers were unable to measure in isolated terms the degree of impact. Thus, their case for moderation in children's programs was weakened. In the recommendations offered by both groups, increased resources for the type of children's programs on public television were strongly advocated.

This should be an interdisciplinary undertaking with psychologists, economists, statisticians, communicators, and engineers involved. Public television licenses held by universities provide a particularly promising linkage between the station and the academic community. I dare say such joint research might enjoy more meaningful application than some now conducted in academic departments.

At the national level, the expansion of research has been an increasing concern at CPB, even though the resources invested must be diverted from direct station support. This is a logical system-wide function of a professional nature for the corporation to perform and should receive larger amounts of support in the years ahead. The corporation's research office was expanded, in 1972, to serve as a clearinghouse for research to be shared with the entire enterprise. One goal was to work toward standardization of questions common to studies in many cities, in order to make results comparable from city to city. This could lead to the development of a central data bank on which all stations could draw. Under the professional guidance of Jack Lyle, a veteran communications researcher, the staff has started to assist stations in planning studies. A pilot project in Jacksonville was designed to measure the effect of the feedback programs broadcast by WJCT-TV. Programs of this type can be the means for greater citizen involvement in the station's service and for the utilization of the medium to foster community dialogue on issues of high local interest.

Field study centers are planned in selected cities, in collaboration with the local station, to provide a continuous measure of the kinds of persons who tune in public broadcasting and their purpose in doing so.

ASCERTAINMENT OF COMMUNITY NEEDS

The phrase "ascertainment of community needs" is a familiar piece of broadcasting jargon. The action the phrase describes is a prerequisite to license renewal for all broadcasters, commercial and public, and periodically surveys and counts are made in the station area to comply. For the most part, this requirement has been accepted as one of the bureaucratic impositions with which broadcasters must live in order to retain that valuable license. In public broadcasting it has an essential meaning. It is a process by which the public station learns the public's needs and interests. The process should receive more frequent and more professional attention. New techniques for ascertainment should be explored. On-air public hearings, mini-town meetings, structured canvasses of major community groups, man-in-the-street interviews, and "stockholder" mailings with proxy questionnaires might all be seriously evaluated by local station leadership. This is a critical area that should actively engage not only the volunteers who work with the station but the members of its board of governors who, by their presence on the board, represent the diverse elements in the community. Of course, such a taking of the public pulse will only breed discontent, unless the results are reported on-air to the participating citizen audience and subsequently the station management reflects these program desires in the broadcast schedule. A special emphasis project should be designed by CPB, NAEB, and PBS on a joint basis, to assist the stations in tangible ways to escertain the views of the publics they serve. Accumulated findings of community needs should be published or broadcast from the national level at least annually, and these findings should be accompanied by evidence of telecast response and specific case examples of particularly significant actions by individual stations.

NEW TECHNOLOGY FOR PUBLIC BENEFIT

Cable television, with its abundance of channels, can enlarge the telecommunication service to the people. Public broadcasting must be alert to this potential and not allow its addiction to over-the-air transmission to restrict its service. The greater flexibility and range of choice in cable-vision can augment and supplement the program material of a public service nature. It can be an even greater asset in reaching isolated communities and in improving an inadequate broadcast signal, particularly from the UHF band. As William Harley, president of NAEB, has proposed, the stations need to be planning to become tele-communication centers for the communities that are pre-pared to use the new technology for improved service. With existing equipment, they can produce programs for transmission at the head end of the cable system. In an expanded capacity, they could become the manager of a cable franchise to assure broad community interest in affording access to these new channels. In yet another role, they can become production contractors for other franchise holders, with obligation to develop locally-originated program services.

But technology extends beyond the cable. Technology now exists to permit a satellite to hang in the sky and provide unimpeded television reception to the entire na-tion. There are currently available a variety of working systems for video cassettes that would allow us to play television programs in our homes the way we now play records or audio tapes. And research is underway into the use of laser beams and holography in television and into the upgrading and improvement of nearly every existing aspect of communications technology, including color telecasting and all-channel television sets. All of these de-velopments can have a major effect on what is or is not available on television sets.

A specific project has been undertaken by HEW and NASA with CPB collaboration. It will result in the use of a new satellite—the Applications Technology Satellite-F—from September 1974 to May 1975. The satellite will ex-plore the technical, economic, and educational practibility of television transmissions to low cost ground receivers in areas of the United States which are difficult or impossible to reach with regular television signals. Specifically, many areas of the Rocky Mountains and the state of Alaska are not now able to receive TV broadcasts. The ATS-F will seek to determine if a special satellite can permit such broadcasts. The goal is to provide such programs as child development, high school science, occupational skills, college courses, and preventive health education. While the results from this experiment are being evaluated, the ATS-F satellite will be moved to a new location from which it can transmit educational programs from a main center in India to five thousand small ground stations located in villages throughout that vast country.

Satellite capability already exists to accommodate the television interconnection. For several years, CPB and PBS have prepared estimates of future interconnection requirements for inclusion in total broadcast needs for satellite service. The FCC has requested prospective satellite operators to present plans for handling public broadcasting in their systems. Although domestic satellite transmission has been delayed by political and economic problems, the first operational systems should be functioning in the next few years. Their utilization may increase the capacity of the public broadcasters to interconnect and to share each other's program resources, and it may reduce the cost of this essential phase in the system.

The public broadcasters must maintain close observation as video cassettes and other modes of television recording evolve from laboratory models to reasonably priced equipment that would give more options to institutions, particularly those in education, in the scheduling and use of video program materials. A number of firms have developed proposed systems, but they differ in design and are not compatible with one another. The retail price of recorders and cassettes or discs is gradually moving within the reach of institutional budgets. The benefits in this form of delivery, in contrast with over-the-air broadcasts, are clearly evident in classroom use. The flexibility in time, the range of options, and the possibility of specially designed material for educational purposes overcome some of the existing difficulties in using broadcast television.

Freed from many of the constraints that inhibit commercial broadcasting, public broadcasting has an obligation to experiment for more effective use of television. High marks for innovation have already been received for such productions as "The Great American Dream Machine," "San Francisco Mix," "Sesame Street," and "The Electric Company." To encourage video experimentation and training in new techniques, CPB has contributed to the support of the National Center for Experiments in Television at KQED in San Francisco. The center has, among other things, developed and put to use a video synthesizer that generates TV images without television cameras. It seeks the capacity of the arts, professions, and other media —such as journalism, radio, film, and theater—to extend the capacity of television beyond the simultaneous transmission of sight and sound.

The application of technology to meet public needs is an imperative for public broadcasting and should not be lost in the recurring crisis over more immediate problems. A capability and an awareness of technical change must be built into the system. The planning process must always receive input from the latest technological advances. Here, again, the national scope of CPB should serve as the constant force for research, planning, and evaluation to assure appropriate system-wide progress.

Without discounting the tension and confusion that may have been generated during these developmental years, the system structure has evolved into a reasonably effective means for operating an unprecedented and complex broadcasting enterprise with multiple parts and divided responsibilities. Some adjustments are definitely required. Some relationships need to be better defined. Some roles need to be more precisely stated. Some strengthening of responsibility for decision making needs to occur. My criticism of the system's performance record is not a manifesto for destruction and rebuilding but rather justification for immediate adjustments to promote more effective service in the future.

At the national level, the concept of CPB as the independent, nonprofit corporation responsible for system development in the broad sense deserves a longer period of testing under conditions of more adequate funding and less political intrusion. Its independence can only be sustained by the attitude and behavior of its board members and its management. The original concept of a nonpolitical board was probably naive once presidential selection and Senate confirmation were required. However, a renewed effort should be directed by the present board to eliminate any tendencies toward political action. Of course, the president's future selections can demonstrate an intent to avoid politicizing through the appointment of more representative members without party involvement or sponsorship. Legislative change to establish longer terms (ten years) and fewer appointments at any one time (two at most to expire the same year) would help to avoid clusters of appointments by the same president in the course of his term. A broader and more representative selection of members from other segments of the American population than those now represented would aid the credibility of the corporation with some groups. Further, the idea of additional station representation might assist in integrating common interests in the system. A step toward this could be accomplished by the appointment of one or two station board chairmen in the next round of selections in 1974.

The tendency of the corporation to drift, to be pushed or to be drawn toward government agency status, should be consciously resisted and arrested by several adjustments:

(1) provide a separate appropriation for CPB, instead of including it as a minor item in the HEW-Labor bill;

(2) permit CPB budget estimates to bypass the president's budget or—where that budget reduces the CPB request—permit the corporation board to present its own requirements to the Congress alongside of the administration proposal;

(3) increase the expectation and expand the quest for funds from nonfederal sources—foundations, corporations, public interest groups, and individuals;

(4) CPB managerial and professional staff should be selected with less emphasis on previous federal government experience and more emphasis on broadcasting, educational, and private background. Special consideration should be given to an increase in assignments at CPB for those with station, regional, or production center involvements;

(5) transfer the educational television facilities pro-

gram from HEW to CPB, to concentrate all federal support within that single nongovernmental agency with an exclusive mission in public broadcasting;

(6) open up CPB board proceedings to the public, permit participation by system and public organization representatives in board policy discussions, and demonstrate the unique role of the corporation in system development;

(7) while exercising accountability to Congress, CPB should also stress its responsibility to all organizational entities in a nongovernmental system composed of independent, nonstandard units;

(8) modify corporation rhetoric to reflect accurately the nondirectional position of CPB in the system; and

(9) give added support to system-wide functions— such as information collection and analysis, research, technology, staff development, community service patterns, program promotion, fund raising—and reduce CPB involvement in program decision making and control over access to interconnection.

If this last adjustment is to be achieved, a new, or a renewed, relationship with PBS must be defined. The original intention for PBS has been reinforced rather than invalidated by recent experience. Through PBS, with its station representation, the program and scheduling views and the standards for production and distribution of programs were formulated with input from across the country. Centralization was only in operating terms, in response to majority opinion communicated from the station level. The drafting and acceptance of standards and procedures was arduous and imperfect, but the process was democratic and had consensus support. The recent decision by the CPB board, to withdraw program-related functions from PBS and to have them performed by CPB staff, should be reversed. This action destroys the delicate system balance, eliminates direct station involvement in essential program decisions, and imposes an overbearing federal presence in the program production and distribution process. The earlier distance between program funding and program coordination and scheduling should be restored, with clearer definition governing the CPB–PBS collaboration. The presumed duplication between the organizations can be eliminated through negotiations based on the objective of removing CPB from direct operations and program development. In the future, CPB should concentrate on system-wide developments, structure standards, procedures, financing, staff quality, technical experimentation, audience research, and program evaluation.

The respective roles of the two organizations should be more precisely defined than they were during my presidency. Then a type of British constitutional situation prevailed as the new agencies gained experience and the decision making was shared on a basis of mutual confidence.

The stations can be effectively involved in the program production and distribution phases of the system through PBS. If that involvement is terminated, the system based on the independence of the stations will not function, and the national services will not fulfill their intended purpose.

It is duplicative as well as unwise for the corporation to devise its own machinery for editorial control over national programs; a balanced system of shared review in accordance with system-developed standards already exists under PBS guidance. The legal accountability under the act can be delegated to PBS under these standards already agreed to by CPB. Federal practice is replete with instances where expenditure decisions are made under delegated authority.

At the meeting of the station managers in April 1972, when future plans for the next five years was the theme of discussion, I called upon all elements in the enterprise to join in "a constitutional convention" to rationalize the system and to reach agreement on the interplay of organizational elements in the operation of the system. Although my historical analogy was overly grand, the need for the action is more critical today than at that time. For future progress there must be means whereby the participative democracy can deliberate and arrive at system judgments that will guide internal behavior and external representation of system views.

The interrelationship of stations, types of stations, regional networks, and trade associations must be spelled out to achieve coherence of action and effective service to the public. In the process, points of responsibility need to be designated and avenues for dissent and disagreement identified for prompt response. Likewise, perhaps mergers or other steps of confederation can be negotiated to simplify public understanding and expedite system operations. The current experience in that task force on long-range financing, with representation of all system elements, suggests a vehicle for this organizational exploration and reordering. Before that group completes its present mission, it should face these problems and determine how continuing joint action might be achieved.

Public television is a complex system. It will not be recast to resemble a commercial network or a foreign broadcast system or a neat, hierarchical business, or government organization. It must function on a shared basis, with all parties contributing to the fundamental policy and operating principles. Preliminary steps for shared decision making in the budget formation process and the construction of criteria for community service grants were affirmative applications of this principle. Statutory rigidities are not the answer for improvement, but system initiated reform should be sought to shape the unique structure so that it is more responsive and responsible, more efficient and creative. The agreements forged out of past internal tensions should be allowed to function for a test period and then be adjusted in accordance with the new organizational pattern, subject to periodic reevaluation. Only a limited start has been made toward a highly decentralized and participative system. Its very uniqueness and absence of precedent makes it difficult to achieve and even more difficult to explain to supporters and critics alike.

NEED FOR UNITY, RESPONSIBILITY, AND CHANGE

To make this system function in a productive and healthy fashion, unity, responsibility, and change must be sought by all elements. Unity, but not uniformity of view, can be the result of shared planning and experience and decision making from a broad base of participation. Responsibility can be reflected in that unity by using existing means for internal debate and position taking. The acknowledged existence of forums for the joining of views can hopefully lessen or at least regularize the tendency toward intramural combat that cripples the system capability to deal with external forces. And the system managers in all elements must be ever willing to accept change when demonstrated weakness, ineffectiveness, or confusion are revealed in the operation of the system.

THE BASIC PRODUCT—PROGRAM

More system attention must be given to the basic product, the TV program of public service. From that basic product, the irrigation system can be constructed to nourish the wasteland until it flowers. More attention will raise the quality of programs and thus cause a general improvement in available TV offerings. Even within existing fund levels, inadequate though they may be, the quest for quality and diversity in programming must be expanded and extended. National leaders should create an atmosphere in which new ideas are nurtured in every category across the wide and diverse range of program opportunities. Where program creativity is found is less important than finding it. The development and presentation of talent in all fields is more important than accumulation of plant and equipment. The possibility of attracting increased funds is enhanced by the presence of talent in writing, producing, performing, and managing. There is no limit on this potential; the ultimate will never be reached. No organization can ever assume that further effort toward this objective is not required. This is the imperative where constructive discontent can prevail in the interest of the public.

But these generalities must be converted to action. Any advocate of public television can compose a one sentence imperative. A veteran of four years exposure to the system should be more specific, even if his action agenda may read like a list of unfinished projects or of broken dreams. Here they are, specific action steps intended to improve the soil and the seed of the wasteland, to strengthen program capacity and broaden the program range:

(1) Despite extended CPB study and planning, no new

educational program has been developed in the interest of adults who desire to expand their learning for employment advancement or personal development. The progress toward this goal should not be sacrificed. The social need remains, and the emphasis on lifelong learning has been magnified. If the direction suggested in the 1971–1972 Adult Learning Program Service (ALPS) project is too ambitious or too expensive, a more modest trial should be arranged to determine how the objective can be pursued more realistically.

(2) The entire area of instructional broadcasting—one-third of the program time—requires national attention, with all elements represented and with educators and technologists joining the discussion. Improvement of product in meeting a variety of educational goals should be possible out of such collaboration. The incorporation of new technology in educational service can readily occur as an adjunct to such a review.

(3) In video journalism, freedom and responsibility are an essential combination. If federal money means a federal editor in charge, the cost is too high. The political reality is that little public affairs programming will be financed by CPB in the next few years. Alternate means, such as the present EEN nightly news project, need to be studied. A cooperative group, supported by station contributions, might contract with NPACT, WNET, or any other production center for journalism projects, to avoid the intrusion of federal control. Such contributions might be augmented by foundation or corporate gifts, with the understanding that the use of those dollars in financing programs is to be unrestricted. If the CPB position in opposition to this area of programming is moderated in the

future, new assurances of independent journalism would have to be secured. The standards and processes previously developed could form the base of journalistic responsibility in conformance with the requirement for fairness, objectivity, and balance.

(4) The access of programs to the interconnection must be guaranteed in an agreement between CPB, PBS, and the producers. Where disagreements arise on allowing specific programs through the interconnection gate, an arbitration process should be devised for resolution in the interest of the system.

(5) More American drama and music should be sought throughout the system and from independent producers on the outside. Talent and production skills should be cultivated in collaboration with universities, conservatories, and foundations. CPB should sponsor gatherings of artists, writers, film makers, and performers to encourage their contributions to public television. Funds for these sessions and for program development should be withheld from support of immediate program production, even if the number of hours of programs transmitted over the interconnection must be reduced.

(6) A systematic review should be conducted of specialized audience groups to identify new target populations for program opportunities. Special features for older Americans, ethnic groups, consumer interests, housewives, physically handicapped, and other clusters by age, interest, ability, and disability should be designed in anticipation of the collective ascertainment of public needs. Where program coverage already exists, as it does for children, future program changes or modifications should be contemplated in anticipation of new interests.

THE IMPERATIVE OF DOLLARS

The imperative of dollars cannot be denied. Costs will continue to rise. The size of the proposed ideal system has generated fund requirements that must be met to complete the national coverage. Although I accept the task force's assumptions, the resulting dollar targets are too high to be realistic, both from federal and from nonfederal sources. A longer and a more deliberate climb must be expected to reach those desired heights. The financial plan for the future should be designed with utmost urgency on the basis of these objectives.

(1) System support should be constructed on multiple financial sources, both public and private, at the local level.

(2) Federal funding should never exceed 40 percent of the total operating expenditures for the entire system; if the total is eventually $300 million, the federal share should not exceed $120 million.

(3) Increased effort, with assistance from CPB and private organizations, should be aimed at achieving a more rapid rise in voluntary contributions from individuals in the form of memberships or gifts. A goal of 25 percent contributors out of the viewer population might be set for these efforts. If a station has a weekly audience of 600,000, it should strive to reach a membership level of 150,000. At an average membership contribution of twenty dollars, this will produce $3 million for discretionary use by station management. Today, a 10 percent membership level has been attained by a very small number of the larger stations.

(4) Federal funding should be provided on a basic matching formula, with an automatic federal matching on a fixed ratio to nonfederal support, public and private,

for the immediate future; the dedicated excise tax should not be discarded as an ultimate objective to be sought after experience with increased voluntary contributions, income from cable subscriptions, application of the matching formula, and other forms of financing.

(5) Expanded program underwriting should be sanctioned and encouraged to augment national program funds. Corporate investment in public television programming can be protected against possible commercialism and should be looked upon as a contribution to public interest accompanied by a legitimate public relations benefit to the contributing company.

(6) Insulation against undue pressures, from whatever source of funding, should be designed and monitored in relation to programming. CPB could expand the insulation by inviting public audit of potential areas of pressure and by periodic open hearings, broadcast over the interconnection, to answer any allegations of interference.

(7) The total financing plan, with detailed specifications and specific steps for achievement, should be completed by an industry-wide body, like the task force on long-range financing. That plan should be reviewed and evaluated periodically to conform with actual developments, new technology, and changed conditions. Once the plan has been matured, it should be presented to governmental representatives in the hope of enlisting their understanding and endorsement.

To secure for the public the benefits of television, to irrigate that wasteland and to realize the service potential of the medium, these imperatives of public involvement, technological pursuit, structural adjustment, programming of higher quality and broader diversity, and financial viability must be the future charter for the system. These

Glossary of Organizational Terms in Public Television

NAEB   National Association of Educational Broadcasters, the trade association and professional society for all educational broadcasters.

ETS/NAEB   Educational Television Stations, division of NAEB devoted to television.

CPB   Corporation for Public Broadcasting, created by Congress in Public Broadcasting Act of 1967 as nonprofit, nongovernmental agency to develop the public broadcasting system in the United States.

PBS   Public Broadcasting Service, created by the educational stations and CPB to manage the interconnection and to coordinate and schedule national programs for distribution on that interconnection.

NET — National Educational Television and Radio Center, created by the Ford Foundation in the 1950s to manage the television program library for educational television stations and subsequently to produce and distribute programming; merged with WNET, Channel 13 in New York, in 1970.

Coordinating Committee of Governing Boards of Public Television stations (no acronym or alphabetical combination attempted), the group of board chairmen formed in 1972 to give stations stronger representation in dealing with CPB, Congress, and the Administration.

ACNO — Advisory Committee of National Organizations, formed by CPB to gain advice of major national groups.

Friends of Public Broadcasting, — Organized volunteers in support of station and system development.

NIT — National Center for Instructional Television, cooperative venture to develop, store, and distribute instructional programs; located at Bloomington, Indiana.

PBL — Public Broadcasting Laboratory (1967–1969), created as an experimental national production center by **Ford** Foundation.

CTW — Children's Television Workshop, established as an independent nonprofit corporation to produce educational programs for children: "Sesame Street" and "The Electric Company."

FCI — Family Communications Inc., the nonprofit corporation formed in Pittsburgh by Fred Rogers in 1971 for the production of "Misterogers Neighborhood" and for research and production of other family-related programs.

WNET, New York — Major program producer, parent for NET in 1970; cultural and public affairs program: "Great American Dream Machine," "NET Opera," "Bill Moyers Journal," "Forsyte Saga," and "NET Playhouse."

WETA, Washington — Major program producer, through NPACT, National Public Affairs Center for Television, video journalism originating in Washington; "Thirty Minutes with ————", Washington Week in Review," "A Public Affair '72" with Vanocur and McNeil, and commen-

tary of congressional hearings and presidential messages.

WGBH, Boston	Major program producer, as licensee for two channels in Boston: "Masterpiece Theatre," "The Advocates" with KCET of Los Angeles, "Zoom," and "Ralph Nader Reports."
KCET, Los Angeles	Major program producer, as licensee for Channel 28 in Los Angeles; drama and public affairs: "Hollywood Television Theatre," "Film Odyssey," and "The Advocates" with WGBH of Boston.
KQED, San Francisco	Major program producer, as licensee for two channels in the Bay Area; public affairs: "World Press," "San Francisco Mix."
WQED, Pittsburgh	Major program producer, as licensee for two channels in Pittsburgh; public affairs, childrens and drama programs: "Turned On Crisis," docudramas, production work for FCI on "Misterogers Neighborhood."
WTTW, Chicago	Major program producer, as licensee for two channels in Chicago, cultural and childrens programs: "Jazz," "Bookbeat," "Kukla, Fran and Ollie."

Appendix A

EEN	Eastern Educational Network
SECA	Southern Educational Communications Association, Inc.
CEN	Central Educational Network
MET	Midwestern Educational Television
RMCPB	Rocky Mountain Corporation for Public Broadcasting
WEN	Western Educational Network
WEST	Western Radio–Television Association

FCC	Federal Communications Commission
HEW	Department of Health, Education, and Welfare
OE	Office of Education, a unit within HEW
NIMH	National Institute for Mental Health, a unit of the National Institutes of Health within HEW.
OTP	Office of Telecommunications Policy
NASA	National Aeronautics and Space Administration

NSF	National Science Foundation
NEA	National Endowment for the Arts
NEH	National Endowment for the Humanities
USIA	United States Information Agency

APPENDIX B

Membership of the Carnegie Commission

James R. Killian, Jr.,
Chairman
James B. Conant
Lee A. DuBridge
Ralph Ellison
John S. Hayes
David D. Henry
Oveta Culp Hobby
J. C. Kellam
Edwin H. Land
Joseph H. McConnell
Franklin Patterson
Terry Sanford
Robert Saudek
Rudolf Serkin
Leonard Woodcock

APPENDIX C

Membership of the CPB Board of Directors

Name	Appointed	Term Expires	Reappointed	Term Expires
Roscoe C. Carroll (R)	3/27/68	3/26/70	No	
Saul Haas (D) Deceased Oct. 1972	3/27/68	3/26/70	Vice Carroll[a]	3/26/76
Erich Leinsdorf (D)	3/27/68	3/26/70	No	
John D. Rockefeller III (R)	3/27/68	3/26/70	No	
Frank E. Schooley (R)	3/27/68	3/26/70	1970	3/26/76
Michael A. Gammino (D)	3/27/68	3/26/72	1972	3/26/76
Oveta Culp Hobby (R)	3/27/68	3/26/72	No	
Joseph D. Hughes (R)	3/27/68	3/26/72	1972	3/26/78
Carl E. Sanders (D) Resigned 6/15/70	3/27/68	3/26/72		
Joseph A. Beirne (D)	3/27/68	3/26/72	No	
Frank Pace, Jr. (D)	3/27/68	3/26/74		
Robert S. Benjamin (D)	3/27/68	3/26/74		

	Nominated		
Jack Valenti (D)	3/27/68	3/26/74	
Milton S. Eisenhower (R) Resigned 1/21/69	3/27/68	3/26/74	
James R. Killian, Jr. (I)	3/27/68	3/26/74	
John Hay Whitney (R) Vice Haas Resigned 5/2/72	9/ 9/70	3/26/76	
Jack Wrather (R) Vice Leinsdorf	8/28/70	3/26/76	
Zelma George (R) Vice Sanders	7/29/71	3/26/72	No
Neal B. Freeman (R) Vice George	6/15/72	3/26/78	
Theodore W. Braun (R) Vice Beirne Resigned 2/21/73	6/15/72	3/26/78	
Gloria L. Anderson (D) Vice Hobby	6/15/72	3/26/78	
Albert L. Cole (R) Vice Eisenhower	3/14/69	3/26/74	
Thomas B. Curtis (R) Vice Whitney	9/13/72	3/26/76	
Thomas W. Moore (R) Vice Rockefeller	9/ 9/70	/3/26/76	
Irving Kristol (D) Vice Haas	1/11/73	3/26/76	

a "Vice" is employed to indicate appointee succeeded by named board member.

Public Television Stations

Alabama ETV Commission
2101 Magnolia Avenue
Birmingham, Ala. 35205

University of Alaska
(KUAC-TV)
College, Alaska 99701

KVZK-TV
Government of American
Samoa
Pago Pago, American
Samoa 96920

KAET-TV
Arizona State University
Tempe, Arizona 85821

KUAT-TV
University of Arizona
Tucson, Arizona 85721

KETS-TV
350 S. Donaghey Street
Conway, Arkansas 72032

KEET-TV
P.O. Box 13
Eureka, California 95501

KCET-TV
4400 Sunset Drive
Hollywood, Calif. 90027

KIXE-TV
P.O. Box 9
Redding, Calif. 96001

KVIE-TV
P.O. Box 6
Sacramento, Calif. 95801

KVCR-TV
701 S. Mt. Vernon Avenue
San Bernardino, Calif. 92403

KPBS-TV
San Diego State College
5402 College Avenue
San Diego, Calif. 92115

KQED-TV
1011 Bryant Street
San Francisco, Calif. 94103

KTEH-TV
70 W. Hedding Street
San Jose, California 95110

KCSM-TV
1700 W. Hillsdale Blvd.
San Mateo, Calif. 94402

KRMA-TV
1261 Glenarm Place
Denver, Colorado 80204

KTSC-TV
900 West Orman
Pueblo, Colorado 81004

WEDN-TV
24 Summit Street
Hartford, Conn. 06106

WETA-TV
2600 Fourth Street, N.W.
Washington, D.C. 20001

WUFT-TV
Room 234, Stadium Bldg.
University of Florida
Gainesville, Fla. 32601

WJCT-TV
2037 Main Street
Jacksonville, Florida 32206

WMFE-TV
2908 W. Oak Ridge Road
Orlando, Florida 32809

WPBT-TV
1410 N.E. Second Avenue
Miami, Florida 33132

WSRE-TV
1000 College Blvd.
Pensacola, Fla. 32504

WFSU-TV
202 Dodd Hall
Florida State University
Tallahassee, Fla. 32306

WEDU-TV
908 S. 20th Street
Tampa, Fla. 33605

WUSF-TV
4202 Fowler Avenue
Tampa, Fla. 33602

WGTV-TV
University of Georgia
Athens, Georgia 30601

WETV-TV
740 Bismark Road, N.E.
Atlanta, Georgia 30324

Georgia ETV Network
1540 Stewart Avenue
Atlanta, Georgia 30310

KGTF-TV
Box 3615
Agana, Guam 96910

KHET-TV
1776 University Avenue
Honolulu, Hawaii 96822

KBGL-TV
Idaho State University
Pocatello, Idaho

KAID-TV
Boise State College
Boise, Idaho 46202

KUID-TV
University of Idaho
Moscow, Idaho 83843

WSIU-TV
Southern Illinois University
Carbondale, Ill. 62901

WTTW-TV
5400 N. St. Louis Avenue
Chicago, Ill. 60625

WTVP-TV
Illinois Valley Public
Telecommunications Corp.
1501 W. Bradley Avenue
Peoria, Illinois 61606

WILL-TV
University of Illinois
Urbana, Illinois 61801

WTIU-TV
Indiana University
Bloomington, Indiana 47401

WFYI-TV
Metropolitan-Indianapolis
Television Association
P.O. Box 880-20
Indianapolis, Ind. 46208

WNIN-TV
9201 Petersburg Road
Evansville, Ind. 47711

WIPB-TV
Ball State University
Box 2701
Muncie, Indiana 47302

WCAE-TV
2152 Moeller Street
St. John, Indiana 46373

WVUT-TV
Vicennes University
Vicennes, Indiana 47591

KDIN-TV
1912 Grand Avenue
Des Moines, Iowa 50307

KTWU-TV
Signal Hill
Wanamaker Road
Topeka, Kansas 66604

KPTS-TV
309 East Third
Wichita, Kansas 67202

WKLE-TV
600 Cooper Drive
Lexington, Kentucky 40502

WKPC-TV
2301 Clarendon Avenue
Louisville, Kentucky

WYES-TV
916 Navarre Avenue
New Orleans, La. 70124

WCBB-TV
Bates College
Lewiston, Maine 04240

WMEB-TV
Alumni Hall
University of Maine
Orono, Maine 04473

WMPB-TV
Maryland Center for Public
Broadcasting
Owings Mills, Md. 21117

WGBH-TV
125 Western Avenue
Boston, Mass.

WMSB-TV
Board of Trustees
Michigan State University
600 Kalamazoo Street
East Lansing, Michigan 48823

WCMU-TV
Central Michigan University
Mt. Pleasant, Michigan 48858

WUCM-TV
Delta Road
University Center, Mich. 48710

WTVS-TV
26945 W. Eleven Mile Road
Detroit, Michigan 48075

West Central Minnesota
Educational Television
Company
128 West Soreson
Appleton, Minn.

WDSE-TV
210 Bradley Building
Duluth, Minn. 55802

KTCA-TV
1640 Como Avenue
St. Paul, Minn. 55103

WMAA-TV
Mississippi Authority for
Educational Television
P.O. Drawer 1101
Jackson, Miss. 39205

KCPT-TV
2100 Stark Road
Kansas City, Mo. 64126

KETC-TV
6996 Millbrook Blvd.
St. Louis, Mo. 63130

Nebraskans For Public
Television, Inc.
P.O. Box 83111
Lincoln, Nebraska 68501

KLVX-TV
5700 Maple Street
Las Vegas, Nevada 89109

WENH-TV
Box Z
Durham, N.H. 03824

WNJT-TV
New Jersey Public Broadcasting
Authority
1573 Parkside Avenue
Trenton, N.J. 08638

KNME-TV
Regents of University of
New Mexico
1801 Roma N.E.
Albuquerque, N.M. 87106

WSKG-TV
Box 954
Binghampton, N.Y. 13902

WNYE-TV
112 Tillary Street
Brooklyn, N.Y.

WNED-TV
Hotel Lafayette
Buffalo, N.Y. 14203

WLIW-TV
Ellington Avenue West
Garden City, N.Y. 11530

WCNY-TV
Old Liverpool Road
Liverpool, N.Y. 13088

WNYC-TV
Municipal Building
New York, N.Y. 10007

WNET-TV
304 West 58th Street
New York, N.Y. 10019

WXXI-TV
410 Alexander Street
Rochester, N.Y. 14607

WMHT-TV
Box 17
Schenectady, N.Y. 12301

WNPE-TV
St. Lawrence Valley Educationa
Television Council, Inc.
P.O. Box 114
Watertown, N.Y. 13601

WUNC-TV
University of North Carolina
Chapel Hill, N.C. 27514

KFME-TV
4500 S. University Drive
Fargo, N.D. 58102

WOUB-TV
Ohio University
Athens, Ohio 45701

WBGU-TV
Bowling Green State University
Bowling Green, Ohio 43402

WCET-TV
2222 Chickasaw Street
Cincinnati, Ohio 45219

WVIZ-TV
4300 Brookpart Road
Cleveland, Ohio 44134

WOET-TV
2470 North Star Road
Columbus, Ohio 43221

WOSU-TV
2470 North Star Road
Columbus, Ohio 43221

WGSF-TV
Newark Public School System
19 N. Fifth Street
Newark, Ohio 43055

WMUB-TV
Miami University
Oxford, Ohio

WGTE-TV
Manhattan Blvd.
at Elm Street
Toledo, Ohio, 43608

KETA-TV
Box 2146
Norman, Okla. 73069

KOKH-TV
1801 N. Ellison Street
Oklahoma City, Okla. 73106

WTVI-TV
42 Coliseum Drive
Charlotte, North Carolina

KOAC-TV
Oregon State System of Higher
Education
2828 S.W. Front Avenue
Portland, Oregon 97201

WLVT-TV
South Mountain Drive West
Bethlehem, Pa. 18015

WQLN-TV
Waterford Pike
Erie, Pa. 16509

WITF-TV
P.O. Box Z
Hershey, Pa. 17033

WHYY-TV
4548 Market Street
Philadelphia, Pa. 19139

WQED-TV
4337 Fifth Avenue
Pittsburgh, Pa. 15213

WVIA-TV
Box 4444
Scranton, Pa. 18509

WPSX-TV
201 Wagner Building
Pennsylvania State University
University Park, Pa. 16802

WSBE-TV
600 Mt. Pleasant Avenue
Providence, R. I. 02908

WRLK-TV
2712 Millwood Avenue
Columbia, S.C. 29205

KESD-TV
South Dakota State Univ.
Brookings, S.D. 57006

South Dakota Educational
Television Board
University of South Dakota
Vermillion, S.D. 57069

KUSD-TV
University of South Dakota
Vermillion, S.D. 57069

WKNO-TV
Memphis State University
P.O. Box 80,000
Memphis, Tenn. 38111

WDCN-TV
Nashville Public Television
Council, Inc.
P.O. Box 12555
Nashville, Tenn. 37212

WSJK-TV
Neyland Stadium
University of Tennessee
Knoxville, Tenn. 37219

KLRN-TV
P.O. Box 7158
Austin, Texas 78712

KERA-TV
3000 Harry Hines Blvd.
Dallas, Texas 75201

KUHT-TV
4513 Cullen Blvd.
Houston, Texas

KTXT-TV
Tech Station
Box 4359
Lubbock, Texas 79409

KNCT-TV
Central Texas College
Killeen, Texas 76541

KWCS-TV
1538 Gibson Avenue
Ogden, Utah 84404

KBYU-TV
C-306 FAC
Brigham Young University
Provo, Utah 84601

KUED-TV
101 Music Hall
University of Utah
Salt Lake City, Utah 84112

WETK-TV
Ethan Allen Avenue
Winooski, Vermont 05404

WNVT-TV
8325 Little River Turnpike
Annandale, Va. 22003

WVPT-TV
Port Republic Road
Harrisonburg, Va.

WHRO-TV
5200 Hampton Blvd.
Norfolk, Va. 23508

WCVE-TV
1904 Old Farm Road
Box 3237
Richmond, Va. 23235

WSVN-TV
Box 15
Roanoke, Va. 24001

KWSU-TV
Washington State University
Pullman, Washington 99163

KCTS-TV
Drama-TV Building
University of Washington
Seattle, Wash. 98105

KPEC-TV
Steilacoom Blvd.
Lakewood, Center, Wash.
98499

KSPS-TV
South 3911 Regal Street
Spokane, Washington 99203

KTPS-TV
P.O. Box 1357
Tacoma, Wash. 98401

KYVE-TV
1105 S. 15th Avenue
Yakima, Washington 98902

WSWP-TV
West Virginia Educational
Broadcasting Authority
1900 Washington St. East
Charleston, West Va. 25305

WMUL-TV
1737 Third Avenue
Huntington, West Va. 25701

WWVU-TV
West Va. University
Morgantown, West Va. 26506

WHA-TV
3313 University Ave.
Madison, Wisconsin 53705

WMVS-TV
1015 North Sixth Street
Milwaukee, Wisconsin 53203

Public Law 90–129
90th Congress, S. 1160
November 7, 1967

An Act

To amend the Communications Act of 1934 by extending and improving the provisions thereof relating to grants for construction of educational television broadcasting facilities, by authorizing assistance in the construction of noncommercial educational radio broadcasting facilities, by establishing a nonprofit corporation to assist in establishing innovative educational programs, to facilitate educational program availability, and to aid the operation of educational broadcasting facilities; and to authorize a comprehensive study of instructional television and radio; and for other purposes.

Be it enacted by the Senate and House of Representatives of the United States of America in Congress assembled. That this Act may be cited as the "Public Broadcasting Act of 1967".

TITLE I—CONSTRUCTION OF FACILITIES

EXTENSION OF DURATION OF CONSTRUCTION GRANTS FOR EDUCATIONAL BROADCASTING

SEC. 101. (a) Section 391 of the Communications Act of 1934 (47 U.S.C. 391) is amended by inserting after the first sentence the following new sentence: "There are also authorized to be appropriated for carrying out the purposes of such section, $10,500,000 for the fiscal year ending June 30, 1968, $12,500,000 for the fiscal year ending June 30, 1969, and $15,000,000 for the fiscal year ending June 30, 1970."

(b) The last sentence of such section is amended by striking out "July 1, 1968" and inserting in lieu thereof "July 1, 1971".

Appendix E

SEC. 102. Effective with respect to grants made from appropriations for any fiscal year beginning after June 30, 1967, subsection (b) of section 392 of the Communications Act of 1934 (47 U.S.C. 392 (b)) is amended to read as follows:

"(b) The total of the grants made under this part from the appropriation for any fiscal year for the construction of noncommercial educational television broadcasting facilities and noncommercial educational radio broadcasting facilities in any State may not exceed 8½ per centum of such appropriation."

NONCOMMERCIAL EDUCATIONAL RADIO BROADCASTING FACILITIES

SEC. 103. (a) Section 390 of the Communications Act of 1934 (47 U.S.C. 390) is amended by inserting "noncommercial" before "educational" and by inserting "or radio" after "television".

(b) Subsection (a) of section 392 of the Communications Act of 1934 (47 U.S.C. 392(a)) is amended by—

(1) inserting "noncommercial" before "educational" and by inserting "or radio" after "television" in so much thereof as precedes paragraph (1);

(2) striking out clause (B) of such paragraph and inserting in lieu thereof "(B) in the case of a project for television facilities, the State noncommercial educational television agency or, in the case of a project for radio facilities, the State educational radio agency,";

(3) inserting "(i) in the case of a project for television facilities," after "(D)" and "noncommercial" before "educational" in paragraph (1) (D) and by inserting before the semicolon at the end of such paragraph ", or (ii) in the case of a project for radio facilities, a nonprofit foundation, corporation, or association which is organized primarily to engage in or encourage noncommercial educational radio broadcasting and is eligible to receive a license from the Federal Communications Commission; or meets the requirements of clause (i) and is also organized to engage in or encourage such radio broadcasting and is eligible for such a license for such a radio station";

(4) striking out "or" immediately preceding "(D)" in paragraph (1), and by striking out the semicolon at the end of such paragraph and inserting in lieu thereof the following: ", or (E) a municipality which owns and operates a broadcasting facility transmitting only noncommercial programs;";

(5) striking out "television" in paragraphs (2), (3), and (4) of such subsection;

(6) striking out "and" at the end of paragraph (3), striking out the period at the end of paragraph (4) and inserting in lieu thereof "; and", and inserting after paragraph (4) the following new paragraph:

"(5) that, in the case of an application with respect to radio broadcasting facilities, there has been comprehensive planning for educational broadcasting facilities and services in the area the applicant proposes to serve and the applicant has participated in such planning, and the applicant will make the most efficient use of the frequency assignment."

(c) Subsection (c) of such section is amended by inserting "(1)" after "(c)" and "noncommercial" before "educational television broadcasting facilities," and by inserting at the end thereof the following new paragraph:

"(2) In order to assure proper coordination of construction of noncommercial educational radio broadcasting facilities within each State which has established a State educational radio agency, each applicant for a grant under this section for a project for construction of such facilities in such State, other than such agency, shall notify such agency of each application for such a grant which is submitted by it to the Secretary, and the Secretary shall advise such agency with respect to the disposition of each such application."

(d) Subsection (d) of such section is amended by inserting "noncommercial" before "educational television" and inserting "or noncommercial educational radio broadcasting facilities, as the case may be," after "educational television broadcasting facilities" in clauses (2) and (3).

(e) Subsection (f) of such section is amended by inserting "or radio" after "television" in the part thereof which precedes paragraph (1), by inserting "noncommercial" before "educational television purposes" in paragraph (2) thereof, and by inserting "or noncommercial educational radio purposes, as the case may be" after "educational television purposes" in such paragraph (2).

(f) (1) Paragraph (2) of section 394 of such Act (47 U.S.C. 394) is amended by inserting "or educational radio broadcasting facilities" after "educational television broadcasting facilities," and by inserting "or radio broadcasting, as the case may be" after "necessary for television broadcasting".

(2) Paragraph (4) of such section is amended by striking out

"The term 'State educational television agency' means" and inserting in lieu thereof "The terms 'State educational television agency' and 'State educational radio agency' mean, with respect to television broadcasting and radio broadcasting, respectively," and by striking out "educational television" in clauses (A) and (C) and inserting in lieu thereof "such broadcasting".

(g) Section 397 of such Act (47 U.S.C. 397) is amended by inserting "or radio" after "television" in clause (2).

FEDERAL SHARE OF COST OF CONSTRUCTION

SEC. 104. Subsection (e) of section 392 of the Communications Act of 1934 (47 U.S.C. 392(e) is amended to read as follows:

"(e) Upon approving any application under this section with respect to any project, the Secretary shall make a grant to the applicant in the amount determined by him, but not exceeding 75 per centum of the amount determined by the Secretary to be the reasonable and necessary cost of such project. The Secretary shall pay such amount from the sum available therefor, in advance or by way of reimbursement, and in such installments consistent with construction progress, as he may determine."

INCLUSION OF TERRITORIES

SEC. 105. (a) Paragraph (1) of section 394 of the Communications Act of 1934 is amended by striking out "and" and inserting a comma in lieu thereof, and by inserting before the period at the end thereof ", the Virgin Islands, Guam, American Samoa, and the Trust Territory of the Pacific Islands".

(b) Paragraph (4) of such section is amended by inserting "and, in the case of the Trust Territory of the Pacific Islands, means the High Commissioner thereof" before the period at the end thereof.

INCLUSION OF COSTS OF PLANNING

SEC. 106. Paragraph (2) of section 394 of the Communications Act of 1934 is further amended by inserting at the end thereof the following: "In the case of apparatus the acquisition and installation of which is so included, such term also includes planning therefor."

TITLE II—ESTABLISHMENT OF NONPROFIT EDUCATIONAL BROADCASTING CORPORATION

SEC. 201. Part IV of title III of the Communications Act of 1934 is further amended by—

    (1) inserting

"SUBPART A—GRANTS FOR FACILITIES"

immediately above the heading of section 390;

(2) striking out "part" and inserting in lieu thereof "subpart in sections 390, 393, 395, and 396;

(3) redesignating section 397 as section 398, and redesignating section 394 as section 397 and inserting it before such section 398, and inserting immediately above its heading the following:

"SUBPART C—GENERAL"

(4) redesignating section 396 as section 394 and inserting it immediately after section 393;

(5) inserting after "broadcasting" the first time it appears in clause (2) of the section of such part IV redesignated herein as section 398 ", or over the Corporation of any of its grantees or contractors, or over the charter or bylaws of the Corporation".

(6) inserting in the section of such part IV herein redesignated as section 397 the following new paragraphs:

"(6) The term 'Corporation' means the Corporation authorized to be established by subpart B of this part.

"(7) The term 'noncommercial educational broadcast station' means a television or radio broadcast station, which (A) under the rules and regulations of the Federal Communications Commission in effect on the date of enactment of the Public Broadcasting Act of 1967, is eligible to be licensed or is licensed by the Commission as a noncommercial educational radio or television broadcast station and which is owned and operated by a public agency or nonprofit private foundation, corporation, or association or (B) is owned and operated by a municipality and which transmits only noncommercial programs for educational purposes.

"(8) The term 'interconnection' means the use of microwave equipment, boosters, translators, repeaters, communication space satellites, or other apparatus or equipment for the transmission and distribution of television or radio programs to noncommercial educational television or radio broadcast stations.

"(9) The term 'educational television or radio programs' means programs which are primarily designed for educational or cultural purposes."

(7) striking out the heading of such part IV and inserting in lieu thereof the following:

Appendix E

(8) inserting immediately after the section herein redesignated as section 398 the following:

"EDITORIALIZING AND SUPPORT OF POLITICAL CANDIDATES PROHIBITED

"Sec. 399. No noncommercial educational broadcasting station may engage in editorializing or may support or oppose any candidate for political office."

(9) inserting after section 395 the following new subpart:

"SUBPART B—CORPORATION FOR PUBLIC BROADCASTING

"Congressional Declaration of Policy

"Sec. 396. (a) The Congress hereby finds and declares—

"(1) that it is in the public interest to encourage the growth and development of noncommercial educational radio and television broadcasting, including the use of such media for instructional purposes;

"(2) that expansion and development of noncommercial educational radio and television broadcasting and of diversity of its programing depend on freedom, imagination, and initiative on both the local and national levels;

"(3) that the encouragement and support of noncommercial educational radio and television broadcasting, while matters of importance for private and local development, are also of appropriate and important concern to the Federal Government;

"(4) that it furthers the general welfare to encourage noncommercial educational radio and television broadcast programing which will be responsive to the interests of people both in particular localities and throughout the United States, and which will constitute an expression of diversity and excellence;

"(5) that it is necessary and appropriate for the Federal Government to complement, assist, and support a national policy that will most effectively make noncommercial educational radio and television service available to all the citizens of the United States;

"(6) that a private corporation should be created to facilitate the development of educational radio and television broadcasting and to afford maximum protection to such broadcasting from extraneous interference and control.

"Corporation Established

"(b) There is authorized to be established a nonprofit corporation, to be known as the 'Corporation for Public Broadcasting', which will not be an agency or establishment of the United States Government. The Corporation shall be subject to the provisions of this section, and, to the extent consistent with this section, to the District of Columbia Nonprofit Corporation Act.

"Board of Directors

"(c) (1) The Corporation shall have a Board of Directors (hereinafter in this section referred to as the 'Board'), consisting of fifteen members appointed by the President, by and with the advice and consent of the Senate. Not more than eight members of the Board may be members of the same political party.

"(2) The members of the Board (A) shall be selected from among citizens of the United States (not regular fulltime employees of the United States) who are eminent in such fields as education, cultural and civic affairs, or the arts, including radio and television; (B) shall be selected so as to provide as nearly as practicable a broad representation of various regions of the country, various professions and occupations, and various kinds of talent and experience appropriate to the functions and responsibilities of the Corporation.

"(3) The members of the initial Board of Directors shall serve as incorporators and shall take whatever actions are necessary to establish the Corporation under the District of Columbia Nonprofit Corporation Act.

"(4) The term of office of each member of the Board shall be six years; except that (A) any member appointed to fill a vacancy occurring prior to the expiration of the term for which his predecessor was appointed shall be appointed for the remainder of such term; and (B) the terms of office of members first taking office shall begin on the date of incorporation and shall expire, as designated at the time of their appointment, five at the end of two years, five at the end of four years, and five at the end of six years. No member shall be eligible to serve in excess of two consecutive terms of six years each. Not withstanding the preceding provisions of this paragraph, a member whose term has expired may serve until his successor has qualified.

"(5) Any vacancy in the Board shall not affect its power, but shall be filled in the manner in which the original appointments were made.

"Election of Chairman; Compensation

"(d) (1) The President shall designate one of the members first appointed to the Board as Chairman; thereafter the members of the Board shall annually elect one of their number as Chairman. The members of the Board shall also elect one or more of them as a Vice Chairman or Vice Chairmen.

"(2) The members of the Board shall not, by reason of such membership, be deemed to be employees of the United States. They shall, while attending meetings of the Board or while engaged in duties related to such meetings or in other activities of the Board pursuant to this subpart be entitled to receive compensation at the rate of $100 per day including travel time, and while away from their homes or regular places of business they may be allowed travel expenses, including per diem in lieu of subsistence, equal to that authorized by law (5 U.S.C. 5703) for persons in the Government service employed intermittently.

"Officers and Employees

"(e) (1) The Corporation shall have a President, and such other officers as may be named and appointed by the Board for terms and at rates of compensation fixed by the Board. No individual other than a citizen of the United States may be an officer of the Corporation. No officer of the Corporation, other than the Chairman and any Vice Chairman, may receive any salary or other compensation from any source other than the Corporation during the period of his employment by the Corporation. All officers shall serve at the pleasure of the Board.

"(2) Except as provided in the second sentence of subsection (c)(1) of this section, no political test or qualification shall be used in selecting, appointing, promoting, or taking other personnel actions with respect to officers, agents, and employees of the Corporation.

"Nonprofit and Nonpolitical Nature of the Corporation

"(f) (1) The Corporation shall have no power to issue any shares of stock, or to declare or pay any dividends.

"(2) No part of the income or assets of the Corporation shall insure to the benefit of any director, officer, employee, or any other individual except as salary or reasonable compensation for services.

"(3) The Corporation may not contribute to or otherwise support any political party or candidate for elective public office.

"Purposes and Activities of the Corporation

"(g) (1) In order to achieve the objectives and to carry out the purposes of this subpart, as set out in subsection (a), the Corporation is authorized to—

"(A) facilitate the full development of educational broadcasting in which programs of high quality, obtained from diverse sources, will be made available to noncommercial educational television or radio broadcast stations, with strict adherence to objectivity and balance in all programs or series of programs of a controversial nature;

"(B) assist in the establishment and development of one or more systems of interconnection to be used for the distribution of educational television or radio programs so that all noncommercial educational television or radio broadcast stations that wish to may broadcast the programs at times chosen by the stations;

"(C) assist in the establishment and development of one or more systems of noncommercial educational television or radio broadcast stations throughout the United States;

"(D) carry out its purposes and functions and engage in its activities in ways that will most effectively assure the maximum freedom of the noncommercial educational television or radio broadcast systems and local stations from interference with or control or program content or other activities.

"(2) Included in the activities of the Corporation authorized for accomplishment of the purposes set forth in subsection (a) of this section, are, among others not specifically named—

"(A) to obtain grants from and to make contracts with individuals and with private, State, and Federal agencies, organizations, and institutions;

"(B) to contract with or make grants to program production entities, individuals, and selected noncommercial educational broadcast stations for the production of, and otherwise to procure, educational television or radio programs for national or regional distribution to noncommercial educational broadcast stations;

"(C) to make payments to existing and new noncommercial educational broadcast stations to aid in financing local educational television or radio programing costs of such stations, particularly innovative approaches thereto, and other costs of operation of such stations;

"(D) to establish and maintain a library and archives of noncommercial educational television or radio programs and related materials and develop public awareness of and disseminate information about noncommercial educational television or radio broadcasting by various means, including the publication of a journal;

"(E) to arrange, by grant or contract with appropriate public or private agencies, organizations, or institutions, for interconnection facilities suitable for distribution and transmission of educational television or radio programs to noncommercial educational broadcast stations;

"(F) to hire or accept the voluntary services of consultants, experts, advisory boards, and panels to aid the Corporation in carrying out the purposes of this section;

"(G) to encourage the creation of new noncommercial educational broadcast stations in order to enhance such service on a local, State, regional, and national basis;

"(H) conduct (directly or through grants or contracts) research, demonstrations, or training in matters related to noncommercial educational television or radio broadcasting.

"(3) To carry out the foregoing purposes and engage in the foregoing activities, the Corporation shall have the usual powers conferred upon a nonprofit corporation by the District of Columbia Nonprofit Corporation Act, except that the Corporation may not own or operate any television or radio broadcast station, system, or network, community antenna television system, or interconnection or program production facility.

"Authorization for Free or Reduced Rate Interconnection Service

"(h) Nothing in the Communications Act of 1934, as amended, or in any other provision of law shall be construed to prevent United States communications common carriers from rendering free or reduced rate communications interconnection services for noncommercial educational television or radio services, subject to such rules and regulations as the Federal Communications Commission may prescribe.

Appendix E

"Report to Congress

"(i) The Corporation shall submit an annual report for the preceding fiscal year ending June 30 to the President for transmittal to the Congress on or before the 31st day of December of each year. The report shall include a comprehensive and detailed report of the Corporation's operations, activities, financial condition, and accomplishments under this section and may include such recommendations as the Corporation deems appropriate.

"Right To Repeal, Alter, or Amend

"(j) The right to repeal, alter, or amend this section at any time is expressly reserved.

"Financing

"(k)(1) There are authorized to be appropriated for expenses of the Corporation for the fiscal year ending June 30, 1968, the sum of $9,000,000, to remain available until expended.

"(2) Notwithstanding the preceding provisions of this section, no grant or contract pursuant to this section may provide for payment from the appropriation for the fiscal year ending June 30, 1968, for any one project or to any one station of more than $250,000.

"Records and Audit

"(l) (1) (A) The accounts of the Corporation shall be audited annually in accordance with generally accepted auditing standards by independent certified public accountants or independent licensed public accountants certified or licensed by a regulatory authority of a State or other political subdivision of the United States. The audits shall be conducted at the place or places where the accounts of the Corporation are normally kept. All books, accounts, financial records, reports, files, and all other papers, things, or property belonging to or in use by the Corporation and necessary to facilitate the audits shall be made available to the person or persons conducting the audits; and full facilities for verifying transactions with the balances or securities held by depositories, fiscal agents and custodians shall be afforded to such person or persons.

"(B) The report of each such independent audit shall be included in the annual report required by subsection (i) of this section. The audit report shall set forth the scope of the audit and include such statements as are necessary to present fairly the Corporation's assets and liabilities, surplus or deficit, with an analysis of the changes therein during the year, supplemented in reasonable detail by a statement of the Corporation's income and expenses during the year, and a statement of the sources and application of funds, together with the independent auditor's opinion of those statements.

"(2) (A) The financial transactions of the Corporation for any fiscal year during which Federal funds are available to finance any portion of its operations may be audited by the General Accounting Office in accordance with the principles and procedures applicable to commercial corporate transactions and under such rules and regulations as may be prescribed by the Comptroller General of the United States. Any such audit shall be conducted at the place or places where accounts of the Corporation are normally kept. The representative of the General Accounting Office shall have access to all books, accounts, records, reports, files, and all other papers, things, or property belonging to or in use by the Corporation pertaining to its financial transactions and necessary to facilitate the audit, and they shall be afforded full facilities for verifying transactions with the balances or securities held by depositories, fiscal agents, and custodians. All such books, accounts, records, reports, files, papers and property of the Corporation shall remain in possession and custody of the Corporation.

"(B) A report of each such audit shall be made by the Comptroller General to the Congress. The report to the Congress shall contain such comments and information as the Comptroller General may deem necessary to inform Congress of the financial operations and condition of the Corporation, together with such recommendations with respect thereto as he may deem advisable. The report shall also show specifically any program, expenditure, or other financial transaction or undertaking observed in the course of the audit, which, in the opinion of the Comptroller General, has been carried on or made without authority of law. A copy of each report shall be furnished to the President, to the Secretary, and to the Corporation at the time submitted to the Congress.

"(3) (A) Each recipient of assistance by grant or contract, other than a fixed price contract awarded pursuant to competitive bidding procedures, under this section shall keep such records as may be reasonably necessary to fully disclose the amount and the disposition by such recipient of the proceeds of such assistance, the total cost of the project or undertaking in connection with which such assistance is given or used, and the amount and nature of that portion of the cost of the project or undertaking supplied by other sources, and such other records as will facilitate an effective audit.

"(B) The Corporation or any of its duly authorized representatives, shall have access for the purpose of audit and examination to any books, documents, papers, and records of the recipient that are pertinent to assistance received under this section. The Comptroller General of the United States or any of his duly authorized representatives shall also have access thereto for such purpose during any fiscal year for which Federal funds are available to the Corporation."

TITLE III—STUDY OF EDUCATIONAL AND INSTRUCTIONAL BROADCASTING

STUDY AUTHORIZED

SEC. 301. The Secretary of Health, Education, and Welfare is authorized to conduct, directly or by contract, and in consultation with other interested Federal agencies, a comprehensive study of instructional television and radio (including broadcast, closed circuit, community antenna television, and instructional television fixed services and two-way communication of data links and computers) and their relationship to each other and to instructional materials such as videotapes, films, discs, computers, and other educational materials or devices, and such other aspects thereof as may be of assistance in determining whether and what Federal aid should be provided for instructional radio and television and the form that aid should take, and which may aid communities, institutions, or agencies in determining whether and to what extent such activities should be used.

DURATION OF STUDY

SEC. 302. The study authorized by this title shall be submitted to the President for transmittal to the Congress on or before June 30, 1969.

APPROPRIATION

SEC. 303. There are authorized to be appropriated for the study authorized by this title such sums, not exceeding $500,000, as may be necessary.

Approved November 7, 1967.

Growth Pattern, 1969–1972

	Fiscal Year 1969	*Fiscal Year 1972*	*Percent Increase 1969–1972*
Number of television stations	150	223	49
Total number of hours broadcast	460,000	720,000	57
System Income	$118,000,000	$229,000,000	94
Interconnection hours per week	10	26.7	167

SOURCE: Corporation for Public Broadcasting Annual Report, 1972.

APPENDIX G

Grade "A" Coverage Populations Public Television Stations, November 1, 1971

	UHF Coverage			VHF Coverage			Total Coverage	
	Stations	Population[1]	%	Stations	Population	%	Population	%
212 public TV stations	90	59.7	100	122	88.5	100	148.3	100
59 community stations	23	31.0	52.0	36	50.4	56.9	81.4	54.9
23 school stations	7	2.9	4.8	16	10.1	11.4	13.0	8.8
68 state and municipal stations	28	11.0	18.3	40	19.7	22.2	30.6	20.6
62 university stations	32	14.9	24.9	30	8.4	9.5	23.2	15.7

[1] Population figures in millions

SOURCE: "A Study on the Financing of Public Television," by Wilbur Schramm and Lyle Nelson, from the Aspen Study on Public Communications, Aspen Study on Communications and Society.

Characteristics of PTV Station Types, 1971

Station ownership	Number of stations	PTV population coverage	Local programming expenditures	Total operations expenditures	Total station revenues
Community	27%	55%	57%	53%	48%
School	11	9	4	8	7
State and municipal	32	20	23	23	27
University	30	16	16	16	18

NOTE: Read this table as follows: 27% of all the PTV stations in the country, as of 1971, were community stations. 11% were owned by school systems. The community stations were responsible for 53% of all PTV operating expenditures; the school stations, for 8%.

SOURCE: "A Study on the Financing of Public Television," by Wilbur Schramm and Lyle Nelson from the Aspen Study on Public Communications, Aspen Study on Communications and Society.

APPENDIX I

US Noncommercial Compared with US Commercial Television Stations

STATIONS	(Financial figures in $ thousands)					
	1966	1967	1968	1969	1970	1971
NONCOMMERCIAL						
Number of stations	113	119	146	189	195	207
Total station revenue	58,315	54,324	66,719	84,928	103,641	141,982*
Mean per station	516	457	457	449	530	686
Total station expense	57,492	62,238	67,091	96,938	107,228	142,838
Mean per station	509	523	460	513	550	690
COMMERCIAL STATIONS						
Number of stations	613	626	655	680	690	695
Total station revenue	1,291,000	1,322,100	1,504,400	1,652,200	1,663,600	#
Mean per station	2,106	2,112	2,297	2,391	2,408	
Total station expense	888,900	963,300	1,066,200	1,191,200	1,259,800	
Mean per station	1,450	1,539	1,628	1,752	1,823	

NONCOMMERCIAL AS A FRACTION OF COMMERCIAL STATIONS

Number of stations	18.4%	19.0%	22.3%	27.8%	28.2%	29.8% #
Total station revenue	4.5%	4.1%	4.4%	5.1%	6.2%	
Mean per station	24.5%	21.6%	19.9%	18.8%	22.0%	
Total station expense	6.5%	6.5%	6.3%	8.1%	8.5%	
Mean per station	35.1%	34.0%	28.3%	29.3%	30.2%	

NOTES:

1. Revenues and expenditures reported are for stations *only*, and do not include network operations.

2. To some extent apparent increases in 1971 PTV station revenues and expenditures are the result of the consolidation of NET operations into New York station WNET/13.

3. If the noncommercial figures were analyzed by *licensees* rather than by *stations*, the revenue and expenditures would in each case be larger, and the difference between noncommercial and commercial stations therefore less than in the table above. Thus, for the last three years (in $ thousands):

	1969	1970	1971
Mean revenue per licensee	690	773	1,068
Mean expense per licensee	788	800	1,074

SOURCES: 1966–1968 figures for noncommercial stations are from the NAEB annual surveys. The 1969–1971 noncommercial figures are from CPB surveys. (The reporting agency for noncommercial station data changed in 1960 from NAEB to CPB. The reporting bases of these two organizations may not be strictly comparable.)

Figures for commercial stations are from FCC annual reports. #FCC figures for 1971 were not yet available at this writing.

"A Study on the Financing of Public Television," by Wilbur Schramm and Lyle Nelson, from the Aspen Study on Public Communications, Aspen Study on Communications and Society.

Sources of Funds By PTV Station Type, 1966–1971, Summary

Sources	Percent of all income for that column classification				
	All PTV stations	Community	School	State and municipal	University
Tax sources[a]					
1966	69.0	39.1	97.8	98.8	91.6
1968	64.4	38.1	93.6	95.9	85.9
1970	62.8	29.4	93.5	95.7	83.3
1971	60.3	23.5	91.3	97.5	86.6
Foundations					
1966	14.4	29.5	0.1	0.3	1.9
1968	9.1	16.7	0.1	1.6	0.4
1970	8.3	15.0	0.2	1.9	4.4
1971	11.2	23.3	0.4	0.2	0.9
Private sources					
1966	10.9	21.4	2.0	0.7	2.1
1968	15.6	28.3	5.2	1.3	2.1
1970	14.3	29.0	2.2	0.5	2.8
1971	13.2	26.0	2.3	0.6	2.8
Public broadcasting agencies and contracts					
1966	–	–	–	–	–
1968	7.3	11.6	0.3	0.2	8.0
1970	11.3	20.2	3.9	1.5	7.6
1971	12.5	22.0	6.0	1.7	7.4
Other sources					
1966	5.6	10.1	0.1	0.1	4.3
1968	3.6	5.4	1.0	0.9	3.6
1970	3.4	6.2	0.3	0.3	2.0
1971	2.8	5.2	–	–	2.3

NOTE: [a] "Tax sources" includes all state and local support, and federal support *exclusive of* that distributed by public broadcasting agencies.

SOURCES: 1970 and 1971 figures from CPB annual surveys. 1966 and 1968 figures from NAEB surveys. "A Study on the Financing of Public Television," by Wilbur Schramm and Lyle Nelson, from the Aspen Study on Public Communications, Aspen Study on Communications and Society.

Public Television Programming Sources, 1971

Program source	Proportion of hours broadcast from each source		
	Total Programming	Programming for Schools	General Programming
Produced locally	23.0%	35.9%	16.0%
Delivered by national interconnection	27.5%	6.9%	38.8%
Delivered by regional interconnection	5.1%	3.2%	6.1%
Delivered by other interconnection	3.9%	5.5%	3.0%
Film and tape distributed from: National Educational Television	6.9%	1.8%	9.7%
Regional networks	5.2%	6.5%	4.5%
ETS/Program Service	3.4%	1.1%	4.7%
National Instructional Television	3.8%	10.6%	0.1%
Great Plains National Instructional Television Library	3.4%	9.0%	0.3%
Other PTV stations	3.3%	5.6%	2.0%
Commercial syndicates	3.1%	0.8%	4.4%
All other sources	11.4%	13.1%	10.4%
TOTAL	100%	100%	100%
Total hours broadcast (193 stations)	639,611	226,165	413,446
Proportion for School & General use	100%	35.4%	64.6%

SOURCE: Corporation for Public Broadcasting, 1971 Survey. Based on 193 PTV stations on the air during the entire 1971 fiscal year. "A Study on the Financing of Public Television," by Wilbur Schramm and Lyle Nelson, from the Aspen Study on Public Communications, Aspen Study on Communications and Society

Television Service Costs by Country

Service	Total ($)	Per person expenditure
CBC (Canada) Television, 1970/71[a] All CBC TV expenditures, including commercial programming	166,583,800	$ 7.70
Parliamentary Grant—Television[b]	123,733,400	5.81
Source: CBC/Société Radio—Canada Annual Report, 1970/71		
BBC (UK) Television, 1970/71 (Totally non-commercial)	183,241,000	3.29
Source: BBC Handbook, 1972, p. 210		
NHK (Japan) Television, 1971/72[c] Estimated TV share of budget	300,000,000	2.90
Source: NHK Handbook, 1971, p. 33		
US Commercial Television Station and Network revenues, 1970	2,808,200,000	13.71
Source: FCC Annual Report, Fiscal Year 1971		
Network revenues only, 1971	1,487,500,000	7.32
Source: FCC Release, May 12, 1872		
US Public Television Total System Revenues, FY 1971	165,632,100	.80
PTV Station Revenues, FY 1971	141,982,200	.69
Source: Corporation for Public Broadcasting		
CPB Federal Appropriation, FY 1972	35,000,000	.17
Appropriation is for the support of public broadcasting, including both radio and television.		

SOURCE: "A Study on the Financing of Public Television," by Wilbur Schramm and Lyle Nelson, from the Aspen Study on Public Communications, Aspen Study on Communications and Society.

[a] CBC operates other broadcasting services in addition to television. Expenditures shown are for direct television costs and a calculated portion of CBC common costs. The CBC TV networks operate as commercial services for parts of each broadcast day.

[b] "Grant" amount shown is net cost to taxpayers, based on calculated television share of total CBC parliamentary grant of $166,000,000 less commercial television revenues of $42,850,000.

[c] NHK operates both radio and television services. Budget amount shown in calculated television portion of total NHK 1971/72 budget of $372,190,000.

Index

Index